D1028830

CHUPACABRA
ROAD TRIP

About the Author

Nick Redfern is the author of more than thirty books on the worlds of the paranormal, the supernatural, and the unknown. His previous titles include *Monster Diary*, *There's Something in the Woods*, and *Monster Files*. Nick has appeared on dozens of television shows, including SyFy Channel's *Proof Positive*, History Channel's *Monster Quest*, Nat Geo WILD's *The Monster Project*, and Fox News. Nick lives just a short drive from Dallas, Texas's infamous grassy knoll. He can be contacted at his blog, *World of Whatever*: http://nickredfernfortean.blogspot.com.

CHUPACABRA
ROAD TRIP

in search of the
elusive beast

Nick Redfern

Llewellyn Publications
Woodbury, Minnesota

FIRST EDITION

First Printing, 2015

Cover illustration: Dominick Finelle / The July Group
Cover design: Kevin R. Brown
Interior photographs provided by the author, except as noted.

Llewellyn Publications is a registered trademark of Llewellyn Worldwide Ltd.

Library of Congress Cataloging-in-Publication Data
Redfern, Nick.
    Chupacabra road trip : in search of the elusive beast / Nick Redfern. —
1st ed.

        pages   cm
    Includes bibliographical references.
    ISBN 978-0-7387-4448-3
    1. Chupacabras. 2. Monsters. 3. Hunting. I. Title.
    QL89.2.C57R44 2015
    001.944—dc23

                                                    2015020763

Llewellyn Worldwide Ltd. does not participate in, endorse, or have any authority or responsibility concerning private business transactions between our authors and the public.

All mail addressed to the author is forwarded, but the publisher cannot, unless specifically instructed by the author, give out an address or phone number.

Any Internet references contained in this work are current at publication time, but the publisher cannot guarantee that a specific location will continue to be maintained. Please refer to the publisher's website for links to authors' websites and other sources.

Llewellyn Publications
A Division of Llewellyn Worldwide Ltd.
2143 Wooddale Drive
Woodbury, MN 55125-2989
www.llewellyn.com

Printed in the United States of America

Other books by this author

Monster Diary

Monster Files

The Bigfoot Book

Contents

Introduction . . . 1

PART 1: THE PUERTO RICAN MONSTER

Chapter 1: A Monster Hunter Is Born . . . 7

Chapter 2: The Proof Is Positively Out There . . . 11

Chapter 3: A Nightmare on the Farm . . . 17

Chapter 4: Horror on the Hills . . . 25

Chapter 5: Monsters in the Rain Forest . . . 31

Chapter 6: A Beast Called Batzilla . . . 37

Chapter 7: Mimicking a Movie . . . 41

Chapter 8: Dealing with Danger . . . 47

Chapter 9: The Road of Terror . . . 55

Chapter 10: Fields Filled with Fear . . . 59

Chapter 11: A Deadly Predator Calls . . . 67

PART 2: THE GOAT SUCKER IN THE UNITED STATES AND MEXICO

Chapter 12: The Elmendorf Beast . . . 73

Chapter 13: The Year of the Chupacabra . . . 83

Chapter 14: The Monster Invades Mexico and My Mailbox . . . 91

Chapter 15: Goat Suckers on the Move . . . 101

PART 3: CHUPACABRA CONSPIRACIES

Chapter 16: The Texas Chupacabra and an Underground Base . . . 111

Chapter 17: Making a Monkey Out of Vampires . . . 119

Chapter 18: Crashed UFOs, a Secret Base,
and a Certain Monster . . . 135

Chapter 19: The Roosevelt Roads Affair . . . 143

Chapter 20: The Chupacabra
from a Land Down Under? . . . 149

PART 4: HUNTING VAMPIRES

Chapter 21: Sacrifice and Vampires . . . 161

Chapter 22: The Moca Vampire . . . 167

Chapter 23: The Village of the Undead . . . 171

Chapter 24: Blood Gets Spilled in Old San Juan . . . 177

PART 5: HOAXES AND MISTAKEN IDENTITY

Chapter 25: "It's Alive!" . . . 187

Chapter 26: An Out-of-Place Predator . . . 193

Chapter 27: Mistaking Bigfoot for the Chupacabra! . . . 201

Chapter 28: A Photograph Falls Flat on Its Face . . . 209

PART 6: FINAL WORDS AND THEORIES

Chapter 29: 2014: A Monster, a Movie,
and Moscow Mayhem . . . 215

Chapter 30: A Bloody Controversy . . . 219

Conclusion . . . 235

Bibliography . . . 239

Acknowledgments . . . 249

Note

The names of some of the people referenced in the pages
of this book have been changed to protect privacy.

INTRODUCTION

Welcome to the Island of Vampires

Puerto Rico is an enchanting and mysterious place. Located in the northeast Caribbean, it comprises the main island itself, plus the islands of Mona, Monito, Vieques, Caja de Muertos, Culebra, and a number of other, smaller bodies. Today, Puerto Rico has a population of close to four million people, while its land mass is of roughly 3,500 square miles.

In the mid-1990s, the phenomenon of the chupacabra exploded all across Puerto Rico. So far as can be determined, the menacing creature first surfaced in March 1995, when numerous animals were found slaughtered in the towns of Morovis (located in central Puerto Rico) and Orocovis, which is situated within the La Cordillera Central mountain range. Locals were plunged into states of near-hysteria by the attacks, which reportedly left animals dead with strange marks on their necks and a distinct lack of blood in their corpses. Since many of the early attacks were on goats, the term "chupacabra" was created and means, in Spanish, goat sucker.

Vampires were on the loose—monstrous vampires. Reports of strange killings soon began to surface from other parts of the island. The creatures were clearly on the move, and the death rate increased even more. The population was on edge and the media had something new and sensational to report on. It was a turbulent and strange time.

But what exactly was responsible for all the killings? Yes, there were plenty of dead animals, but unfortunately there was no solid, eyewitness testimony about the killers themselves. That is, until August 1995, when a woman named Madelyne Tolentino, who lived in Canovanas, close to the northeast coast of Puerto Rico, changed everything. Tolentino's description of the creature she encountered close to her mother's home was disturbing, to say the least. It was a description eagerly embraced by the island's media and by investigators of monsters and mysteries.

Tolentino told journalists and researchers that the creature was around three feet in height, bipedal, ran in a weird, hopping fashion, had large black eyes, bony fingers on each hand, overly long arms and legs, and a kind of feathery line running down its back. Or it appeared to Tolentino to be a feathery line; a young boy employed by Tolentino's husband claimed that he saw the beast up close and maintained that the feathers were, in reality, sharp spines. The boy also said that the creature possessed a mouthful of vicious-looking fangs. Not only did the people know of the chupacabra and its predations, they also now knew what it looked like—something straight out of their worst nightmares.

As the years progressed, so did the attacks. And what was, for a while, a mystery of purely Puerto Rican proportions very soon became global. Within twelve months of the chupacabra surfacing in Puerto Rico it appeared in Mexico. Then, as the 1990s came to a close, the focus was on Brazil: blood-drained farm animals were found strewn across Sorocaba, Sao Paulo. Just a few months later, Chile was hit hard by the beast, which reportedly killed not dozens but hundreds of animals. Texas became a favorite haunt of the chupacabra in 2004. Even Russia got in on the act in the 2000s. The chupacabra was no longer just a mystery. It was a veritable planetary phenomenon.

But what is the truth of the creatures? Are we really dealing with a deadly group of blood-sucking monsters who have now spread across the world, killing and violating as they see fit? Could the answers be found in the domains of the occult, the paranormal, and the supernatural? Are the animals the results of top secret genetic experiments? Is it possible that pollution and subsequent mutation play roles in the story? Is the phenomenon purely mythological? Might there actually be multiple explanations for what's going down? These, and many more, are questions that I have pondered deeply. I have also done my utmost to answer them.

Part 1

THE PUERTO RICAN MONSTER

Chapter 1

A MONSTER HUNTER IS BORN

My interest in strange creatures and monstrous animals dates back to my early childhood. When I was just six years old, my parents took me on a two-week holiday to Scotland. While there, we spent a day at one of the most mysterious places on the planet. You surely know the one: Loch Ness. Even today, I still have a few memories of my father telling me the story of the Loch Ness Monster—far better known, of course, as Nessie. As we stood on the shores of the huge loch, surrounded by gigantic, sloping hills and centuries-old castles, I stared intently into the ink-black waters.

I was both amazed and excited at the prospect of a colony of monsters lurking deep within the depths of the mysterious loch. In mere moments, my life was forever changed. I was hooked. I began reading books on the likes of Bigfoot, sea serpents, the Abominable Snowman, Mothman, werewolves, and just about each and every other winged, scaled, hair-covered, or long-necked monster that was said to inhabit the darker corners of our world. And, sometimes, the not-so-darkened corners too.

When I left school, I began working on a magazine titled *Zero*. It was a publication dedicated to rock music, fashion, celebrity gossip, and much more, and catered to the people of the English town where I was then living. I embraced the world of journalism like an old friend and, after a few years, elected to combine my experience in the domain of writing with that of monster hunting.

Since that formative, fateful day at Loch Ness, I have traveled the world in search of those creepy creatures that science and zoology assure us don't exist, but which thousands of witnesses strongly suggest otherwise. I have pursued wolf-men across the woods of Louisiana, Sasquatch in the vast forests of Washington State, diabolical goatmen throughout Texas, giant birds in the mountains of Mexico, and huge, mysterious black cats deep within the green, sprawling fields of the U.K. It's fair and accurate, however, to say that some of my most memorable pursuits have been of the distinctly undead kind. That's right, we're talking creatures of the night: malignant bloodsuckers. In short—vampires.

Something monstrous and vampiric lurks in the
wilds of Puerto Rico.

Investigating the Undead

Mention of the "V word," for most people, will provoke imagery of decades-old movies featuring the likes of Bela Lugosi and Christopher Lee (as Bram Stoker's famous creation, Count Dracula); the *True Blood*–style vampires, which are far more likely to resemble a combination of Marilyn Manson and Rob Zombie than they are an old guy with a long, black cloak and slicked-back hair; and the almost-zombie-like bloodsuckers of the latest television hit, *The Strain*. And let's not forget the watered-down, anorexic-looking vampires of *Twilight*, which are the absolute antithesis of what any self-respecting vampire should ever aspire to be. So much for on-screen, fictional vampires; my interest, however, is in their real-life counterparts. Specifically, one counterpart: the chupacabra.

Over the years, countless words have been written on the legendary goat sucker. Numerous theories and explanations abound. However, what you are about to read is my own quest for the truth. For a decade, I have pursued the chupacabra with vigor and determination, with nothing more than a wooden stake, a silver cross, and garlic.

This is my story.

Chapter 2

THE PROOF IS
POSITIVELY OUT THERE

April 23, 2004, was a day that I will always remember. Around 11:00 a.m., I received a phone call from a researcher with a newly planned series from the SyFy Channel. I am used to getting calls and e-mails from companies wishing to hire me to appear on their shows, but this one was a bit different. Actually, it was a lot different.

Generally speaking, my TV work falls into two categories: head and shoulders interviews undertaken in darkened, back-lit studios; and a day (or two at most) of on-location shoots in dense woods. But not this one. The show, *Proof Positive: Evidence of the Paranormal*, was downright ambitious, in every sense of the word. The plan was to travel to various locations, some faraway and exotic, in pursuit of strange and paranormal phenomena. I was casually asked if I would be interested in flying to Puerto Rico for a week or more to film an episode on the chupacabra—and for a decent fee too. No prizes for guessing the answer to that question! There was, however, one stipulation: there had to be some kind of evidence that could be forensically analyzed by a team of scientists the SyFy Channel would be bringing on board.

Forensic evidence—what did they mean by that? I asked the researcher, somewhat puzzled. The answer was simple: a bit of hair from a Bigfoot, a piece of debris from a crashed UFO, a claw from a Chupacabra, and so on. The answer may have been simple, but securing the kind of unique evidence that the SyFy Channel had in mind was going to be far from simple. It was going to be pretty much impossible! Or was it? I had a sudden brainstorm and asked the researcher if I could call him back in an hour or so, as I just might have something along the very lines he was thinking of. It was time to put in a quick, transatlantic call to one of my closest friends, way over on the other side of the pond.

From Chupacabra to Chicken

Jon Downes is the director of the Center for Fortean Zoology (CFZ), one of the very few full-time groups in the world that investigates mystery animals. And he's quite a character, too. Try and imagine a swirling combination of Indiana Jones, Hunter S. Thompson, and Rubeus Hagrid from the *Harry Potter* novels and movies, and that's Jon. British-born, six feet five inches tall, wild bearded and equally wild haired, Jon grew up in Hong Kong, where his father was a distinct bigwig in the British government. Jon was educated at one of England's finest schools, has a brother in the British Army who was decorated by Queen Elizabeth II herself, and lives in a centuries-old stone abode in the ancient English county of Devon, where Sir Arthur Conan Doyle set his classic Sherlock Holmes novel *The Hound of the Baskervilles*. All of which is in very sharp contrast to my solidly working-class, beer-swilling, Friday-night-fighting-in-the-pub background in central, industrial England.

Nevertheless, when Jon and I first met, in the summer of 1996, we quickly became firm friends, chiefly as a result of our love of wine, women, and song. We spent the best parts of several years working together on books and TV productions, hanging out at conferences, and generally getting into more than a bit of trouble along the way. But there was something else.

Back in 1998, Jon, along with his sidekick in the CFZ, Graham Inglis, traveled to both Puerto Rico and Mexico with a film crew from Britain's Channel 4. The purpose was to make a television documentary on the chupacabra controversy titled *To the Ends of the Earth*. Although they didn't find the creature, Jon and Graham were able to bring back to England a not insubstantial number of feathers, purloined from the bloody carcass of an unfortunate Puerto Rican chicken that was said to have been violently sliced and diced by a chupacabra. The word on the grapevine was that the feathers were positively soaked in chupacabra saliva. And saliva meant nothing less than DNA. And DNA was precisely the kind of thing the *Proof Positive* people needed to analyze, right? Right!

I phoned Jon and told him what the SyFy Channel had told me. The good news was that Jon still had the feathers, and he was definitely up for a new expedition to Puerto Rico; he suggested I pitch the feathery idea to the channel. I quickly thanked Jon, hung up, and dialed the number I had been given. The game was almost afoot, to slightly mangle the words of a famous, fictional detective of 221b Baker Street, London.

In mere hours there was good news: the *Proof Positive* team loved the idea. Due to the complexities of getting everything arranged, however, it was a full three months after I got the call that Jon and I finally took to the skies for Puerto Rico— me from Dallas-Fort Worth International Airport, and Jon from London's Heathrow Airport. Now the game really was afoot.

Welcome to Puerto Rico

Although Jon and I were flying into Puerto Rico from distinct- ly different parts of the world, our arrival times were barely a couple of hours apart. I was the first to hit the island, after a fun flight of margaritas and music. My contact at Puerto Rico's Luis Munoz Marin International Airport was a woman named Caro- la. I knew next to nothing about her, except that she had almost singlehandedly located all of the interviewees Jon and I would be speaking with. She was responsible for keeping everything mov- ing and on time, and would be holding a big sign reading *Nick Chupacabra*, which I found very amusing.

When I exited the doors of my terminal, which was abso- lutely heaving with people, I was hit by a wall of heat, the likes of which I had never known before, not even in Dallas, Texas, where I live. I can cope with temperatures in the high nineties, but one hundred and ten-plus is too much, even for me. Jon had warned me about this just a couple of days earlier, since he had grown up in the tropics and knew very well the roast- ing fate that awaited me. I took a long swig of water, a deep breath, wiped my already soaking brow, and wandered around for a few minutes.

As Jon gleefully likes to point out, I am a pale Brit and there- fore one who by definition does not fare at all well in really extreme climates. And, indeed, that much became abundantly evident as I fought my way through the crowded exit doors of the airport, as the heat pummeled me squarely in the face like a rock.

I thought, bloody hell, we don't have temperatures like this back in Birmingham—in reference to my home city in the far cooler climes of jolly old England, where I resided until midway through 2001, when I moved to the United States. Nevertheless, I was a man on a mission, and I was not about to let a bit of sun get the better of me. There were monsters to be found, old friendships to be rekindled, new ones to be made, and adventures to be had. Suddenly, I heard someone shout my name. It was Carola, a smiling blonde of about twenty-five.

We shook hands, headed out to the parking area, and jumped into Carola's vehicle. Our destination was the Wind Chimes Inn, which turned out to be an expertly restored colonial villa in Condado, a small community in San Juan of six thousand people. The hotel was located just one block from an amazing beach and seemingly never-ending blue ocean waters. With a large, gated, white wall surrounding it on all sides, a courtyard filled to the brim with palm trees and exotic plants, a large swimming pool, an open-air restaurant, and a well-stocked bar, the Wind Chimes Inn was the perfect place for us. We would spend the evening coordinating our activities, chilling out, and having a damn good time, all the while preparing to chase down hordes of infernal vampires.

As soon as I was checked in, I wandered downstairs and Carola motioned me over to a couple of guys she was speaking with in the lobby. They were our director and cameraman. With greetings exchanged, Carola was airport bound again, this time to meet Jon. She waved and smiled as she shot down the street, dodging tourists, locals, and wild dogs, of which there were dozens roaming around. Since it would be about two hours before Jon arrived, I did the only thing I could: I hit the bar and ordered a frozen margarita. And then, just for good measure, I ordered another.

It turned out that Jon's flight was slightly ahead of time and, as a result, we were soon catching up in person for the first time in nine months. Although we spoke on the phone regularly, I hadn't seen Jon since we spent a weekend lecturing, when not carousing, in Las Vegas, Nevada, in October 2003. It was just like old times. Our cameraman and director were a genial duo, and several hours were spent with them planning the week ahead of us. The bar closed promptly at 11:00 p.m. and so we all retired to our respective rooms, more than satisfied with how things had gone that night.

What had begun, back in April, as a transatlantic phone call about saliva-coated chicken feathers was now a fully fledged operation to find a blood-sucking beast of the rain forest.

Chapter 3

A NIGHTMARE ON THE FARM

Around 7:15 a.m. the following morning, I knocked loudly on Jon's door. A few, mumbled, near-intelligible words were the only things that were offered in return. I told Jon that we were all meeting downstairs in around forty-five minutes. Cue yet further unfathomable mumblings.

I headed downstairs and to the splendid courtyard where breakfast was served every morning. Shortly after, Jon arrived. Dressed in a white dinner jacket, a matching white panama hat, and black trousers, he looked as if he had strode straight out of the pages of Graham Greene's novel *Our Man in Havana*, a comedic and classic 1958 tale of espionage and spies set in Cold War–era Cuba. All that was missing, I thought, was a loaded .45 hidden in the inside pocket of Jon's jacket. I, meanwhile, was in cargo pants and a black T-shirt. The production team was immensely pleased by our respective, and very different, appearances. And so, for the entire week, that was our wardrobe whenever the cameras were rolling—and also when they weren't.

After a hard day of vampire hunting,
a welcome stretch of beach awaits.

We all knew that with punishing temperatures being par for the course, it was vital to get plenty of food and liquid inside us before we tackled whatever it was that each day might bring. Running out of energy and keeling over headfirst would not be good when you're miles from civilization. And, right after breakfast, we soon found ourselves deep in the wilderness of a boiling hot island dominated by vampires.

Things began not unlike a military invasion. Maps were laid out on the breakfast tables. The crew was running around, loading equipment into two large trucks that sat outside the hotel, half blocking the street, frustrating more than a few people who were clearly trying to get to work. Cellphones were ringing left, right and center. The other guests looked on, astonished and puzzled, and wondered what on earth was going on. In the middle of all the anarchy, Jon and I sat back, drank our hot tea, and watched, somewhat amused by the chaotic atmosphere that was exploding all around us. Then, suddenly, we got the call to hit the road. Our quest to uncover the truth of the Puerto Rican bloodsucker was about to begin.

Carola had arranged for Jon and me to have our own transportation. She did not disappoint in the slightest; she got us just about the coolest silver jeep you could imagine. It was, Jon and I joked, our very own equivalent of the Mystery Machine —the trusty van that kept Scooby, Shaggy, Fred, Daphne, and Velma on the road when they were in hot pursuit of everything supernatural. We dropped our rucksacks in the back, climbed in, and waited. Not for long, though. Shortly after 9:00 a.m. our considerable convoy of a jeep, a pair of trucks, and two cars was ready to move.

Jon Downes hangs out in the jeep, as we prepare to hunt for blood-sucking creatures.

Fighting to the Death

We learned that our first interviewee was to be a rancher named Jorge. I imagined him having the kind of huge, sprawling ranch that I was accustomed to seeing in and around the Dallas area, filled with horses and cattle. Well, it wasn't quite like that. It didn't take long for me to realize that Puerto Rico was very much a two-tiered nation. There were the very rich and there were those who nearly endlessly bordered upon downright poor, and there was only a sorely limited amount of room for anything in between. Jorge's ranch was basically the cramped backyard of his tiny home, which was situated in a small village, one that was dominated and surrounded by an amazing rain forest environment. There was not a single horse or cow in sight. What were in sight, however, were chickens—dozens and dozens of them. Jorge was a breeder of chickens used strictly for one of Puerto Rico's most popular and controversial pastimes, cock fighting. Introduced to the island by Spaniards in the 1500s, cock fighting was recognized as a sport in 1770. It remained precisely that until the U.S. invasion of the island in 1898, when it was quickly outlawed. Of course, that didn't stop illegal cock fighting from continuing behind closed doors. Such was the ongoing enthusiasm for cock fighting, its official, legal status was renewed in 1933.

I wasn't—and I'm still not—someone who thinks that seeing animals killed or injured purely for the fun is cool and entertaining. And neither was Jon. We were both acutely aware, however, that we were guests in a foreign land. As a result, we had no right to question the actions of people whose culture was very different from ours, even if we didn't agree with those actions. So Jon and I focused on our reason for being there, which was the matter of a strange series of attacks on Jorge's chickens back in either 1997 or 1998; he wasn't quite sure when.

Blood Draining Beneath the Stars

Since Jorge didn't speak English, we had someone at hand who could do all of the translating. The story that Jorge told was as bizarre as it was uncanny. During the early hours of a summer's morning, Jorge was suddenly woken up by the cries of his chickens, clearly scared out of their wits. Had Jorge checked on the chickens right there and then, the outcome would likely have been different. To his cost, however, Jorge did not. It was not until daybreak that he decided to see what had gone down just a few hours earlier.

The scene before him both shocked and puzzled Jorge. Every single one of his chickens was dead. The killings did not look like the work of a wild animal, however. Indeed, the animals were not torn apart in the slightest, as one might well expect in a ferocious wild dog attack. In fact, the only evidence of damage to the bodies was—wait for it, and take a deep, long breath—a pair of significantly sized holes in the necks of each and every chicken.

Oh, and lest I forget, all the birds were drained of blood, said Jorge. It was at this point that Jon began to make dark and disturbing murmurings about vampirism, black cloaks, fangs, and terrible creatures of the night. It all made for excellent footage for the SyFy Channel. But were the chickens actually drained of blood? Jorge's line of thinking was that because there was a complete lack of blood at the scene, and his cursory study of several of the bodies revealed no blood around the wounds, he had assumed the blood was drained. One could, however, make a very good argument that the blood had sunk to the lower parts of the body, which most assuredly does happen upon death. It's all due to nothing stranger than good old gravity.

I did not know it at the time, but this issue of blood draining, in relation to alleged chupacabra attacks, was one that would dog me for years to come.

The matter of the blood aside, there were undeniable anomalies in the case. Jorge's chickens did not run free in his yard, either during the day or at night. Each chicken had its very own cage, which was kept securely locked at all times. Whatever had killed the birds had opened the latches that kept the doors solidly in place. We said for the cameras that this suggested a human was the guilty party. We also noted, however, there were major flaws in this theory. If a person was responsible, how on earth had they managed to kill more than two dozen chickens in the dead of night and in a very precise fashion, in a remote little village that lacked any streetlights and any other kind of nighttime illumination?

Jon asked Jorge if he had found any footprints, human or otherwise, around the cages, beyond his own. The answer was a decisive no. Jorge did state, however, that he found some rather unusual, coarse hairs stuck in the wires of one particular cage that had been violently twisted out of shape. He told us that the hairs had been handed over to a policeman who promised to have them analyzed. Jorge heard nothing more from the officer and could not recall his name. End of story. Well, not quite. I asked Jorge who or what he thought was responsible for the mass slaughtering. His one word answer was, of course: chupacabra.

I have to say that Jorge's story definitely caught my attention. It was one thing to read about the exploits of the blood-sucking beast in a magazine or a book, and from the comfort of my couch at home. It was quite another, however, to find oneself deep in the heart of the mystery, and perhaps even right in the territory where a deadly creature of murderous proportions had once lurked and killed.

We all thanked Jorge, jumped into our respective vehicles, and hit the road. It was time to get stock footage of Jon and me roaming around dense forests, wading across streams and flowing rivers, wearing facial expressions that varied from amazement to puzzlement, and burning large amounts of rubber in the jeep. As Jon took photos from the passenger seat, I wondered if there was a way I might be able to smuggle this nifty silver machine off the island and back to Dallas while no one was looking. Probably not, but it was definitely something worth thinking about.

Chapter 4

HORROR ON THE HILLS

The next stop on our quest for the truth was a ranch high in the Puerto Rican hills. The drive was an infinitely slow one; practically the last five miles were undertaken on a dirt-filled, track-like road that had nothing but a sheer, three to four hundred foot drop on its right side. A pale-faced Jon repeatedly advised me to drive as carefully as I conceivably could. I did my best to do exactly that and to prevent us from tumbling to our deaths in the dense, jungle-like environment far below.

We were due to meet another rancher whose bad luck it had been to encounter a chupacabra. Unlike Jorge's, this ranch was massive. A large stone house, protected by a tall, cemented white wall, stood firm and proud. A rolling and flowing landscape, huge peaks, and thick woods were all the order of the day.

It turned out that as well as having a huge herd of cattle and numerous goats and pigs, the rancher, Dominic, kept peacocks. And, back in 1998, something very strange happened to some of his brightly plumed birds: four of them were killed during the early hours of a July morning by a stealthy and deadly predator.

The peacock: A victim of the chupacabra.

The modus operandi was by now more than familiar to Jon and me. All four birds displayed evidence of vicious bites to the neck. There was, however, something else too, something that neither of us had seen or heard of before—the skulls of the unfortunate birds had been penetrated by something small and triangular in shape. Dominic, who cared greatly about his peacocks, had quickly hired a veterinarian to examine the corpses. Two of them were subjected to necropsies, which confirmed the animals were lacking in significant amounts of blood. It looked as if our old friend, the chupacabra, had been up to its deadly tricks again. But the best was still yet to come.

Angered at the deaths of his prized peacocks, Dominic elected to keep a very careful watch on his remaining birds. This involved staying up all night and ensuring that there were no repeat attacks. Thankfully, there weren't. But, as Dominic told us, a deadly chupacabra did make a return visit; in fact, it made several visits. We asked Dominic how he could be so sure, if there was no evidence of further attacks and killings. The answer was one that we were very pleased to hear: he had seen the monster for himself.

This was a major development. Here was a highly credible source, one who had the presence of mind to have his dead peacocks examined by a veterinarian, and who, while protecting his remaining birds throughout the course of the night, came face to face with the killer culprit. Dominic was asked to describe what he saw. The peacocks, said Dominic, were housed in a large, fenced enclosure, a fence that on the night of the killings had been violently ripped open on its north-facing side. Since the birds were more like pets than farm animals and were treated as such by Dominic, he decided to take a chair and a flashlight and spend a few nights in the enclosure, in the event that there was a repeat attack. It was a most wise decision.

Confronting a Chupacabra

On the very first night after the attacks, and well after midnight, the creature returned, via the same gaping hole in the fence. When Dominic heard the unmistakable sound of something forcing itself through the opening, he suddenly turned his flashlight in the precise direction of the damaged fence. He was shocked to see a large creature, around four feet in length and tan in color. Initially, said Dominic, the animal walked on all fours, but when hit by the bright beam, it reared up onto its hind legs. As it did so, the beast let out a menacing growl and a large row of spikes suddenly sprung erect down the length of its neck and back. Worse still, the white eyes of the animal suddenly turned to a glowing red. "Devilish" scarcely began to describe the fraught situation.

The scene of the slaughter.

Frozen with fear in his chair, Dominic didn't even make a move to pick up the rifle that sat next to him. The peacocks were screaming at the top of their lungs. Dominic was struck dumb. And, amid all of the chaos and terror, the chupacabra stood its ground, swaying menacingly from side to side as it hissed malevolently at the terrified rancher. Thankfully, however, the creature seemed not to want to tackle a fully grown man, and it suddenly dropped to all fours and charged out of the hole in the fence. While the creature never again bothered Dominic's peacocks, he had no less than four or five more sightings of the animal. They all occurred around dusk, over the next two or three weeks, near his huge field of plantains. On each occasion, the creature beat a hasty retreat into the depths of the field. Dominic never thought to take even a single, solitary photo, which was frustrating for us, to say the least. After that, nothing at all. The killer vanished and was never seen again.

Blood, Peacocks, and a Schizophrenic

It's interesting to note that peacocks crop up in more than a few tales of the unexplained kind. In ancient Babylonian, Greek, and Persian lore, the peacock was seen as an immortal creature, one whose flesh was rumored never to decay, even after death. Such beliefs were later incorporated into Christian beliefs, to the extent that the "eyes" in the tail feathers of the peacock are said to represent the eyes of God.

How curious, Jon and I mused, as we scanned the sprawling ranch before us, that peacocks are linked to beliefs in immortality. Here we were, in the heart of Puerto Rico, searching for a vampire—another creature of perceived immortal proportions, and one that back in 1998 had dined on the blood of no fewer than four peacocks. Had we not known better, both of us might have thought there was something unique about the blood of the peacock, something that could offer nothing less than everlasting life to the imbiber. Such an idea was, of course, nonsense. But that didn't take away the profoundly weird nature of the situation in which we found ourselves.

Moving on, in the summer of 2006, a number of peacocks were found dead in and around a crop circle that appeared overnight in a field in the English county of Staffordshire. The location was right next to an old and ruined, twelfth century structure, Chartley Castle. I know this for sure, as I had the opportunity to personally examine both the circle and the remains of the peacocks, just two days after the formation was found. Rumors were rife within the local villages that occultists had sacrificed the peacocks as part of some disturbing ritual that had at its heart immortality.

And still on the matter of immortal vampires and peacocks, on the morning of June 28, 2007, a peacock turned up in a decidedly unusual location, right outside a Burger King on Staten Island. The astonished staff fed it pieces of bread, all of which were apparently enthusiastically chomped down. But not for long. As if out of nowhere, a wild-eyed man loomed into view and proceeded to beat and throttle the bird, which was so traumatized it had to be put to sleep by a veterinarian. The man in question was a young schizophrenic who had stopped taking his meds. In his deranged state, he believed that the peacock was nothing less than a vampire—an immortal, soulless monster.

To this day, I still remember phoning Jon when the Staten Island story broke. Neither of us could fail to note that this was yet another example of how the peacock and the world of never-ending life, a typical and classic attribute of the vampire, had crossed paths in a curious and fatal fashion.

Back in July 2004, however, Jon and I were still oblivious to what both 2006 and 2007 would bring, and so we got on with the job at hand, doing our utmost to bag ourselves a bloodsucker, whether living, dead, or undead.

Chapter 5

MONSTERS IN THE RAIN FOREST

There comes a time in the life of every investigator of the paranormal when a case just gels. From the credibility of the witness to the importance of the story, everything combines in the best fashion possible. I have experienced such a deep sense of satisfaction and connection on a number of occasions. But there is perhaps no greater example than the amazing affair of a woman named Anna, which came our way on the fourth day of our beastly trek. Anna was a fascinating lady, who lived in a spacious and atmospheric house high in the El Yunque rain forest. Anna's story was one that took our quest for the truth about the chupacabra to a whole new and largely unanticipated level.

After we devoured breakfasts fit for a king in the open courtyard of the Wind Chimes Inn, our convoy of jeep, cars, and trucks once again hit the road. There were people to interview, creatures to be sought, and absolutely no time to waste. Around ninety minutes after we left bustling San Juan behind us, we arrived at

Anna's lavish home. It was dominated by a pair of huge wrought-iron gates and a driveway that was so steep I had to put the jeep in the lowest possible gear to successfully climb it. I quipped to Jon that the fortified home had probably been built to keep the chupacabra out. Who knows? After digesting what Anna said, I seriously had to wonder if my joke just might have been on target after all.

Anna, seventy-something and sporting a beaming smile, invited us in as if we were old friends. It almost felt like we were. Anna was an incredibly generous host, despite unfortunately being in failing health. She provided us with liquid refreshment and snacks, gave us a tour of her home, which was essentially built solidly into the hill on which it stood, and regaled us with entertaining stories of her youth, during which she was a prize-winning, passionate motorcyclist. Both Jon and I instantly bonded with Anna, who was a fellow adventurer and lover of life, and a highly skilled artist too.

Roughly an hour after arriving, the crew had set up all of their equipment, the cameras were ready to roll, and Jon, Anna, and I assumed our required positions on the balcony of Anna's home, which provided an incredible, panoramic view of El Yunque. Indeed, the angle of the miles-wide view, coupled with the sheer altitude of Anna's home, provoked a slight sense of vertigo. But that was no matter. Jon and I suspected that Anna had something special to say and we wanted to hear it. We weren't entirely sure how special, but we quickly found out.

Jeepers Creepers!

Anna's words demonstrated that the chupacabra enigma was much older than many researchers had assumed or concluded.

Anna's account, we were fascinated to learn, dated from 1975, at the height of the summer months.

The defining event itself was actually the culmination of a series of disturbing attacks on domestic animals in the area in which Anna lived. Tragically, this included an assault on one of Anna's pet dogs, which was found dead outside the perimeter of her hillside home. It was also found lacking each and every one of its bones, including its skull, no less. How the bones had been savagely removed was something that not even local veterinarians were able to explain. Other families in the area reported their dogs missing, too. They also were left with nothing but tears, anguish, presumed dead pets, and a mountain of unanswered questions. As circumstances would have it, only a couple of weeks later, Anna had an encounter of a kind that would have made horror maestro H.P. Lovecraft nod approvingly.

It was dusk on a stiflingly hot, weekday night in August 1975. The atmosphere, as day began to surrender to nightfall, was as normal and tranquil as it had ever been. It wasn't long, however, before normality and tranquility gave way to something hideous. As Anna drove carefully and slowly along the twisting, climbing road (in a car, rather than on one of her trusty motorbikes, I should stress), something suddenly surfaced from the huge, dense trees that stood proud and tall, like gigantic green curtains, and which dominated each side of the road.

Doing barely twenty miles an hour to begin with, Anna was easily able to slow down as a curious beast loomed into view. As she looked into the camera, Anna said that only about twenty feet in front of her was the strangest, most terrifying animal it had ever been her misfortune to encounter. For all intents and purposes, it looked very much like a bat. Except, that is, for one astonishing thing: the abomination was around four to five feet in height.

Not surprisingly, Anna could scarcely believe her eyes as the monster shuffled slowly across the road, its muscular legs taking slow but deliberate strides across the hot tarmac. With her eyes transfixed on the beast, Anna could see that its body was dark brown in color. Two large wings were folded tight against its back. The clawed fingers on its hands, which drooped in curious, limp fashion from its bony wrists, were of a distinct, white-yellow hue. Of a near-identical color were two enormous fangs that protruded from its gaping, almost slack-jawed, mouth. Most frightening of all to Anna were the eyes of the creature, which focused intently on Anna herself; they were almost blazing, like red-hot coals.

After what seemed like a torturous amount of time, but which was maybe no more than twenty or so seconds, the creature unfurled its wings. At this point, Anna could see just how big those mighty, membranous appendages were, somewhere in a combined region of twelve to fifteen feet. Anna said the wings flapped in a fast, furious, and loud fashion that deeply shocked her. In mere moments, the beast took to the skies, vertically, and was quickly lost from sight. It was, I said to Jon later, almost a case of the *Jeepers Creepers* movies come to life. He didn't disagree in the slightest.

Since this was the only interview planned for that day, there was no need for us to make a hasty drive to new destinations, and so we hung out for another hour or so, chatting further with Anna, even though the cameras had stopped rolling. Jon and I were suitably impressed. Our quest for the truth of the chupacabra had taken a major step forward and, in terms of the date of Anna's encounter, a major step backwards! And there was one more thing: Anna had so enjoyed the afternoon that she surprised me by presenting me with nothing less than a full-color painting she had done of the creature she encountered back in 1975. I thanked Anna for her incredible generosity. Atmospheric and captivating, her artwork has pride of place on the one wall of my office that is not dominated by mountains of bookshelves.

Chapter 6

A BEAST CALLED BATZILLA

Anna's observations that the animal she was unfortunate enough to encounter on a lonely, winding road late one night back in the summer of 1975 was very much bat-like in appearance led Jon and me to give serious consideration to an intriguing possibility. It was a possibility that suggested the chupacabra was exactly what it appeared to be: a form of giant bat, one not acknowledged to exist by mainstream science and conventional zoology. Well, neither Jon nor I could ever be considered even remotely conventional or mainstream, so thinking definitively outside of the box was fine by both of us. And by "giant bat" we were talking mega-sized. Or, as Jon memorably preferred it, Batzilla, so christened by Jon, paying homage to the world's most famous city-destroying monster, Godzilla.

That Puerto Rico is home to a large population of bats is not a matter of any doubt at all. In fact, "large" is an understatement of epic proportions. For example, Cucaracha Cave alone, which is situated south of the city of Aquadilla, in the Cordillera Jaicoa, is home to quite literally hundreds of thousands of bats. Roughly seventy-five percent of them are Jamaican long-tongue bats, while the remainder are the imaginatively and colorfully named sooty moustache bats and Antillean ghost-faced bats.

Taking into consideration the huge number of additional caves that exist throughout the island, one soon begins to realize just how incredibly widespread the bat is in Puerto Rico. Problematic is the fact that the bats of Puerto Rico are nowhere near the size of the beast encountered by Anna, all those years ago. But was it possible, I wondered, as we drove back to the Wind Chimes Inn Inn after the working day was finally done, that Puerto Rico had in its midst other kinds of bats, those of a truly monstrous type that had yet to be formally classified? That was the controversial question dominating my mind.

Sweat-soaked and grubby from a day clambering through the depths of the El Yunque rain forest, Jon and I both took very welcome showers on our return to the inn. Then, having freshened up, we hit the bar for the evening. It was a night spent hanging out, drinking beer with tequila chasers, and devouring our plentiful meals of good, solid Puerto Rican cuisine. And it was all courtesy of a rapidly growing tab that was due to be picked up by the SyFy Channel at the end of the week, or so we earnestly hoped and prayed. (For those who may be wondering—yes, they did, thankfully.)

Over dinner we mused further upon the Batzilla theory. Whether it had any merit or not, the idea that Puerto Rico had a resident population of grossly oversized, unfriendly bats was so engaging that I could not afford to dismiss it. As we chatted, Jon and I agreed on two things: Puerto Rico clearly was swarming with bats, and the island's network of caves was gigantic.

On this latter point, and as just one example of many, the Camuy River Cave Park (so named after the municipality of

Camuy, situated north of mountainous Lares) comprises almost eleven miles of caverns and more than two hundred caves. Rather significantly, and as I learned to my great surprise, even at the dawn of the 21st century, the cave system was barely explored and mapped. Certainly, skilled cavers conclude to this day that the park is home to hundreds of additional caves that very likely still remain untouched and uninvestigated by anyone. That other portions of the caves were, and still are, closed to the public, thanks to the actions of Puerto Rican authorities, led the conspiratorial side of my mind to wonder just what savage things might be lurking in those out-of-bounds, underground realms.

But what of the possibility of an unknown type of bat, one with a body-length somewhere in the region of four to five feet, living, breeding, and feeding in distinctly stealthy fashion in Puerto Rico? Was it truly feasible? If so, might occasional sightings of the beasts be responsible for the legends of those deadly creatures that had become known as the chupacabras?

A Bloody Mystery

There are large bats out there, even if they don't reach the scale of the creature encountered by Anna. Take, for example, the giant, golden-crowned flying fox (otherwise known as the golden-capped fruit bat). This impressively proportioned beast has a wingspan that can, incredibly, reach five and a half feet. And that makes for a hell of a big bat!

There were a couple of problems, however. First, the flying fox in question lives exclusively in the Philippines and dines on fruit, not on copious amounts of goat blood nor, in fact, on the blood of anything. Second, despite its impressive wingspan, the creature does not have a particularly large body, and certainly not one anywhere near the size of a small human, as Anna had suggested was the case in her encounter. Vampire bats (*Desmodus rotundus*) do partake of blood and voraciously so, to the extent that close to two million livestock lose their lives to these real-life bloodsuckers every single year. The deaths are not, however, due to the bodies of the animals being systematically drained of blood. The cause, chiefly, is disease spread by the bat as it feeds on its prey, most commonly rabies and Venezuelan equine encephalomyelitis.

So, did this mean the theory lacked any and all merit? Well, just maybe not. As we ate our dinner, I had a story to share with Jon that I knew he would find interesting. And he did.

Chapter 7

MIMICKING A MOVIE

In September 1959, a groundbreaking paper was published by the acclaimed scientific journal *Nature*. Its title was "Searching for Interstellar Communications." The authors were two physicists, Phillip Morrison and Giuseppe Conconi, both of Cornell University. In essence, the paper was a study of how microwaves might be successfully used to seek out alien intelligences in other parts of the universe. It had a great effect on one Frank Drake, a man who, after having carefully read the report, embarked on a life and career to search the universe for aliens. Drake began his work at the West Virginia–based Green Bank National Radio Astronomy Observatory. He was, without doubt, the star of the Search for Extraterrestrial Intelligence (SETI) conference that was held at the observatory in October 1961. Drake ultimately gravitated to Puerto Rico, home to the Arecibo Observatory, of which he became the director.

Midway through the 1960s, something decidedly strange happened at the observatory, something that may well have a direct bearing upon the chupacabra phenomenon. A guard reported

seeing a curious character roaming around the edge of the installation. What made the man, if a man it was, so curious was his
long, black cloak. The guard, apparently, had his own ideas on
what he was seeing: one of the undead, a vampire. A report on
the affair was prepared for Drake's attention. That was far from
being the end of the matter, however.

Forty-eight hours after the sighting, Drake said: "I really was
forced to look into it … because a cow was found dead on a nearby farm, with all the blood drained from its body. The vampire
rumor had already spread through the observatory staff, and
now the cow incident whipped the fears of many people into a
frenzy."

Parallels with Hollywood Horror

When I shared this story with Jon, and his mind filtered the data,
you could have heard the veritable pin drop in the Wind Chimes
Inn. There were several things that stood out for me. First,
there was the age of the case. The 1960s was years, decades, to
be correct, before the chupacabra was on anyone's radar. Hell,
it even predated Anna's 1975 account by around ten years. Second, there was the matter of the slaughtered cow being drained
of blood, as in totally drained of blood. And if a man of Drake's
standing and credibility said the body lacked all of its blood, then
it's pretty much a given that this was the case. Third, Drake acknowledged that the death had provoked a "vampire rumor" in
the area, one which all of the observatory staff knew about and
that had whipped up the terror levels of what were specifically
described as "many people." And, finally, there was the matter of
that strange character dressed in a black cloak.

What if, I suggested to Jon, the cloaked man was actually nothing of the sort? What if it was a huge, human-sized bat? And what if the black cloak was, in reality, the massive wings of some monstrous, fiendish bat, one ingeniously camouflaging itself as a human? Certainly, at a distance and late at night, it might be extremely difficult to tell one from the other. I had a good reason for bringing this up. In a somewhat related fashion, a 1999 horror movie hit on very similar territory. Its title was *Mimic*.

The movie, starring Mira Sorvino, Jeremy Northam, and Josh Brolin, is set in New York and tells the story of man-sized, mutated cockroaches that live deep in the city's old train tunnels, and which prowl the darker parts of the Big Apple by night, feeding on anyone and everyone that gets in their way. And how do they manage to successfully move around in the darkness of the city without being detected? With great ease, that's how. They wrap their wings around themselves, mimicking (hence the title of the movie) the gait and stance of someone dressed in a long black trench coat. To be sure, it's eerie to see these shuffling, darkened, upright monsters lurking in the shadows of New York's alleyways, just waiting to pounce on the unwary and the vulnerable. I saw *Mimic* when it was first released and I couldn't help but think that what we had here in Puerto Rico was a classic case of truth being stranger than fiction, to the extent that, in a weird way, it almost mirrored it.

Jon found it all very fascinating, but was not quite as excited as I was by the possibility that this just might explain the monster legend. The bat connection to the mystery beast was not yet over, however. Just one day later, there was a memorable development in this strange saga. Before that, however, there was more tequila to be drunk. Far more. The SyFy Channel's bar tab grew bigger and bigger.

Heading for Trouble

It was around noon the following day when we arrived at the next location on our list of places to explore. It was an impressively sized cavern filled with numerous, smaller, tunnel-like offshoots that extended who knows how far into the huge, green hillside that dominated the amazing scenery. Mysterious caves, angular shadows, lush foliage, the potential for something unspeakable to be hiding in the darkness, and a multitude of bats hanging directly from the ceiling above us were all the order of the day. As the sheer multitude of little critters crawled around, the rocky walls and canopy seemed to mutate into a writhing, swirling, black mass made of something unspeakable and foul. For the film crew, it was a dream come to life. Not for me, however.

As we stood in the cave, I felt something splash against the side of my head. I thought, what the hell was that? I rubbed my head with a towel I kept in my backpack to keep the sweat away. It turned out that a bat had chosen my head as the ideal spot to urinate upon! Unsurprisingly, everyone laughed. And so did I!

Until, that is, someone pointed out that it might be a very good idea if I got a rabies shot, and quickly too. Well, I thought about it, actually, more than several times that day and in the immediate days that followed. I decided, however, to take my chances. After all, it wasn't as if any of the offending liquid had entered my mouth or ears. Plus, I didn't have any open wounds. I never did bother to get the shots. Luckily, I didn't get rabies either.

The infamous cave where I almost contracted rabies.

With that unfortunate encounter out of the way, I returned to the shoot, at which point Jon and I were filmed discussing the possibility that the many and varied caves in Puerto Rico just might make ideal places for a great number of chupacabra to dwell during the day, before going on their nighttime slaughtering and rampaging in the lowlands, the villages, and the farms.

With the cave shoot finally over, Jon and I returned to our trusty jeep. I deliberately spun the wheels as I pulled away, something that overjoyed the crew, who caught it on film. We were headed for pastures and adventures new. As we drove, the two of us continued to ponder on the bat theory, or as some might very well suggest, the batty theory. We mused on whether or not Puerto Rico, against just about all the odds, was playing host to a colony or several of goliath-like bats that lived on the blood of goats, chickens, pigs, and cows.

Jon said he bloody well hoped not, as he gave me a quick, sideways glance.

Chapter 8

DEALING WITH DANGER

By now, you might assume that the most hazardous things in Puerto Rico are the chupacabras. You would, however, be very wrong. Should you venture into certain less-than-safe areas of the island, you'll find that the human population can be far more deadly than that legendary vampire; that is, unless you go prepared for action of the dicey kind. I found this out, and graphically so, on the very last night of our time in Puerto Rico.

Back in 1998, when Jon and Graham Inglis traveled to both Puerto Rico and Mexico in search of the chupacabra, Jon met with a man who worked for what at the time was known as the State Agency of the Civil Defense. Today it's called the Puerto Rico State Agency for Emergency and Disaster Management. A man with a broad knowledge of the chupacabra, he proved to be a valuable source of contacts and information. We were both very pleased to learn that the film crew had arranged for us to meet up with the very same man, who had agreed to be interviewed about his personal investigations.

It was late in the afternoon when we met with him. He instantly remembered Jon. Bear hugs were exchanged between the pair. The man proved to be an excellent interviewee. He discussed for the cameras his thoughts on the chupacabra, his involvement in officially investigating chupacabra attacks for the SACD, and the fact that in one 1998 case he had personally been involved in there had been massive blood loss in three slaughtered goats on a Canovanas farm. When the filming was over, the man took us to one side. He told us that we might like to meet a guy who lived in a village called Villa sin Miedo, situated near Carolina, on the northeast coast of Puerto Rico.

The guy in question had very clear photographs of chupacabra tracks, reportedly found on farmland in Villa sin Miedo itself. We were given a name, an address, and a phone number. Coupled with the fact that we had a detailed map of the island, finding the man was not going to be a problem at all. When the filming was finally over, at around 6:30 p.m. on day six, we headed off to the village to see if we could get our hands on the allegedly priceless imagery. Just as we were about to leave, Jon's old friend warned us to keep our guard up at all times: Villa sin Miedo (which translates into English as "the town without fear"), we were told, was one of the most notoriously dangerous parts of Puerto Rico. The man was not wrong, as became apparent in mere hours.

A Town in Turmoil

The story of Villa sin Miedo is a strange and controversial one. Years earlier, hundreds of homeless people essentially claimed the area for themselves. At the time, it was pastureland owned by the government of Puerto Rico, but which had largely been abandoned. At first, officialdom turned a blind eye to what amounted to large-scale, illegal squatting on the land. The people formed a self-governing community, a community that was the only place in Puerto Rico where drug-based crime was nonexistent. They began to grow their own food. A doctor's office was built. A school soon followed. All was going well, for a while.

Despite having largely ignored what was afoot, the government eventually decided that a self-sufficient community, one that operated outside of the rules and regulations of officialdom, was not something it wished to encourage among the people of Puerto Rico. The result was both tragic and outrageous. One fateful night, the government sent in hundreds of troops and police, armed to the teeth with guns and teargas, and forced all of the villagers to flee for their lives. Then, when daylight broke, bulldozers were sent in to flatten every building. And, to ensure that nothing escaped the carnage, the area was then systematically torched.

The people of Villa sin Miedo proved to be a hardy bunch, however. They returned, regrouped, and rebuilt. They are still there to this day. Unfortunately, the earlier, prosperous days did not return. Villa sin Mideo was blighted by poverty. Further intimidation from the authorities only made things worse. And a rise in crime and violence led the area to gain a notorious reputation, something that Jon and I soon realized.

A Deal for Vampire Evidence Turns Sour

When we finally hit the road to Villa sin Miedo, it was after 8:00 p.m. The atmosphere was sticky and muggy, and the entire landscape was by now enveloped in darkness. And by darkness, I mean it was black. There wasn't even a single streetlight to be seen anywhere. We had a tremendous view of the star-filled heavens above, but also a sense of having suddenly left twenty-first century civilization far behind us. As I concentrated on driving along the precariously narrow roads and tracks, I handed my cellphone to Jon, who called the number given to us by his source in the old SACD. The man with the photographs, whose name it may not be wise for me to mention (even after the passage of more than a decade), was home and was agreeable to a meeting. Well, if nothing else, that was encouraging. It turned out to be the only encouraging thing about the entire night.

As we reached Villa sin Miedo, I just knew we were heading for trouble; you could practically taste it. Only a five-minute drive from where I grew up in the English village of Pelsall is an area known locally as Poets Corner. It takes its name from the streets that make up the area: Shakespeare Crescent, Chaucer Road, and Keats Road are just three of them. It's an area notorious for crime, muggings, car theft, and burglaries. I said to Jon that I had a feeling Villa sin Miedo was Puerto Rico's very own Poets Corner. Jon then proceeded to tell me the history of the Burnt House Lane district of the city of Exeter, a city on the outskirts of which Jon lived for many years, which had a near-identical, notorious reputation.

It's not my intention to badmouth another people and another culture, but everything about Villa sin Miedo set alarm bells ringing loudly in my head. Huge rats patrolled the shabby streets, not unlike some 1950s era New York street gang. The only things the rats seemingly lacked were slicked-back hair, flick knives, and black leather biker jackets. We passed two recently burned-out cars. That much was evident from the still present noxious odor of smoldering metal that lingered in the stifling air. God knows if the drivers made it out alive. As we reached a crossroads and tried to figure out which way we should turn, a skinny, bedraggled, bearded man of about forty approached us with his thin right arm stretched out. Since our jeep had an open top, we didn't hang around to see what he wanted. Money or food, we figured.

Finally, we reached the home of the guy with the photos. A gang of about six men, varying in age from their twenties to their fifties, were sitting in deck chairs in the front yard. All of them were dressed identically, in black pants and white, sleeveless vests. Two sported bandanas; the rest, like me, were shaven-headed. They all eyed us shiftily. A pair of pit bulls, both of them tethered by ropes, barked and growled furiously in our direction as we exited the jeep. I could tell that Jon thought this was not a good idea at all; he didn't even have to say the words. I was inclined to agree, but since we were here, I figured we might at least see where things were going to lead.

From Monster to Alligator

Thankfully, the windows of the building were open and the interior light finally provided us with some very welcome illumination. Before we even had a chance to introduce ourselves, a greasy, fat guy of about sixty strode out of the shadows and said that he wanted two hundred dollars for the photos. I replied that we weren't handing over anything, never mind two hundred dollars, until we saw what he had on offer. For a moment or two there was a silent, tense standoff. I stood my ground, Jon scanned the area for a quick getaway point, and finally our source headed back into the dilapidated house. Within thirty seconds, he was out again. He thrust into my hands a filthy manila envelope. I opened it less than eagerly. Yep, there were the photos. And they did show prints. They were not, however, chupacabra prints. The photos were of something else entirely—an alligator.

The print of an alligator, identical to the alleged
chupacabra photos that almost cost Jon and me our lives.

I said to the man that we were going to call our boss at the television company. I simultaneously pointed in the direction of the jeep. He nodded, somewhat warily, and then shouted in my direction, wanting to know if I had two hundred in cash on me. Well, I was hardly going to answer a question like that! As Jon and I walked the sixty or so feet to the jeep, I showed him the photos. He concurred that they showed nothing stranger than an alligator. And Jon made a good point: who could say the pictures were even taken in Puerto Rico? Then I heard a sound that was unmistakable: it was the cocking of a pistol, right in the yard we had just exited. That was a very bad development. As we sat in the jeep, Jon tried to phone the television crew but couldn't get a signal, which was an even worse omen. I had visions of us being robbed at gunpoint, or worse.

At that point, out of the darkness, an elderly man came up to us, almost out of nowhere, it seemed. As the gang of six or seven watched from their chairs, he told us in quiet and concerned tones that we should leave the area, as in immediately. What had begun as an adventure was now quite possibly a life and death situation.

I threw the envelope about ten feet in the direction of the man's home, turned on the ignition, and floored the accelerator. Complete and utter uproar broke out, as the gang jumped out of their chairs and raced in our direction. We about made it out of the narrow, rat-infested street unscathed. Thankfully, we were not followed. But, for good measure, I turned off the jeep's headlights for about the next ten minutes of the journey.

Eventually, the bright and beckoning lights of Old San Juan appeared on the horizon and we knew we were safe. Less than an hour later, Jon and I were sitting in the bar of the Wind Chimes Inn, laughing at our brush with death, and toasting our lucky escape from a man and his posse, who tried to convince us, for a two hundred dollar fee, that an alligator was a vampire. He failed.

From Goodbye to Broadcast

That was not only the night that saw Jon and me narrowly avoiding a distinctly bad fate in a dark, menacing, Puerto Rican town. It also marked the end of our weeklong time pursuing the chupacabra. I was due to fly back to the United States early the next morning, one day before Jon headed back to England. So, after finally completing what I like to call Project Chicken Saliva, we all had a final dinner in San Juan, toasted to friendships old and new, quaffed endlessly to a job well done, and said our farewells.

Jon aside, I have never seen any of the other *Proof Positive* crew again. They are, today, more than ten years later, merely the stuff of memories and faces on old photographs. However, I will never forget that week in the summer of 2004, when I roamed Puerto Rico's rain forest, its lowlands, and its little villages in search of the chupacabra. It was an experience that will stay with me for all of my life, and one that was as much about friendship, adventures, and good times as it was about hunting for the chupacabra. And at the end of the day, that was good enough for me.

A few months later, the episode of *Proof Positive* for which we were filmed finally aired. I remember sitting on my couch with a fair degree of anticipation as the minutes and the seconds counted down to the broadcast. I have done television shows (both before and since) that proved to be cringe-worthy in the extreme. This one, however, was much different. There had been no attempt on the part of the editors to make Jon and me look ridiculous (some might say we do a good enough job of that all by ourselves), and the story was told pretty much as it occurred, the time constraints permitting.

Unfortunately, the one piece of evidence that just might have solved the mystery, the chicken feather, had degraded to such a degree since 1998 that nothing incriminating or out of the ordinary was found by the forensic team that the SyFy Channel had hired to examine it. Never mind. I would have further chances to crack the mystery wide open. My quest for the truth about the chupacabra had scarcely begun.

Chapter 9

THE ROAD OF TERROR

While I was in Puerto Rico in the summer of 2004, I gave my phone number to all of the Puerto Rico–based crewmembers on the *Proof Positive* shoot, just in case any of them got any leads of the chupacabra variety. Late one morning not long after I returned home, I received a phone call from a woman I'll call Rosa. I listened intently as Rosa told me how, on a Friday night around thirteen years previously, she was having a night on the town in Old San Juan with one of her girlfriends. The evening was normal, fun, and just like any Friday night anywhere on the planet. At least, until they decided to head home.

For reasons which neither Rosa nor her friend could ever fathom, both developed a sudden and overpowering urge to drive to El Yunque. It was, said Rosa, as if the pair was in a kind of hypnotic haze. Around 1:00 a.m. they arrived at the base of the rain forest and took a long and winding road, one that I know very well, into its depths. They had driven along the compact, coiling road for around fifteen minutes when they encountered something that was as remarkable as it was terrifying: a very strange animal making its slow way across the road.

Whatever the creature was, it was certainly no regular resident of Puerto Rico. Somewhere in the region of four-and-a-half feet in height, colored gray, it moved across the road in a curious, tentative fashion, as if, said Rosa, it wasn't even used to walking, and sported a pair of what were undeniably wings on its hunched back. The wings, she added, were so long, they dragged on the ground for a couple of feet behind the beast. There was one more thing: the animal had a pair of self-illuminating red eyes. That much was apparent when it stopped in its tracks and gave the friends an icy stare, after which it continued on its odd, clumsy, penguin-like walk to the left side of the road and vanished into the trees.

Things were not quite over, however. With the creature now gone, Rosa and her friend slowly came out of the odd, hypnotic state that had caused them to drive into the heart of El Yunque at such an odd hour. Rosa had an intriguing, but also unsettling, explanation for what had happened. She felt that, somehow, the beast had compelled them to drive to the location, specifically to ensure they saw it; although Rosa admitted she had no idea, at all as to why it would have done such a strange thing. There was only one thing, Rosa said, that she knew for sure, and that was that she encountered a chupacabra years before the 1995 wave began, as had Anna in 1975. And speaking of Anna, I couldn't fail to notice the truly astonishing parallels between her sighting and that of Rosa's.

Interestingly, yet another winged thing was encountered in Puerto Rico, this time in the mid-1990s at Guánuca Lagoon. The creature, rather notably, was described as having bat-like wings and had attacked not only farm animals but people, too. Supposedly, its lair was a long-abandoned sugar mill and specifically its old tunnels. Very significantly, a police officer said that although he had not seen the monster, while on patrol in the direct vicinity of the old mill he "heard the beating of powerful wings, as if something was propelling itself off the zinc roof of one of the mill's cranes."

Death at the Zoo
and a Diabolical Monster

In the same week that the *Proof Positive* show hit the SyFy Channel, Puerto Rico's Illusion Park was hit by a series of vicious deaths. The park, located in the Montehiedra Town Center in Rio Piedras, was home to a small zoo that contained numerous animals which the local kids loved to visit and pet. Fausto Radaelli was the owner of the park. He was also the man who, early one morning as he arrived for work, was confronted by a scene of carnage: nearly a dozen goats had been killed overnight. The attacker was never identified. He, she, or it did, however, leave a chilling sign, as the *Primera Hora* newspaper of December 3, 2004, revealed:

> Three of the goats presented large bite marks, dis-
> memberment, and one of them had half of its body
> devoured; all of its internal organs, excepting its stom-
> ach, were gone. The rest of the goats had bite marks
> and fang marks on the rear of their bodies. The marks
> resembled the ones found on animals allegedly attacked
> by the infamous chupacabra.

Not everyone was quite so sure that the chupacabra was the cause of the deadly devastation. A local biologist named Ernesto

Marquez told the newspaper that the most likely cause of the deaths was "a wolf, a coyote, a hybrid, or very large feral dogs." Commenting on the teeth marks present on the dead goats, Marquez said, "These are regular fang marks. Canids kill animals by the rear, seizing them to hold them down and eat them. The animal leaped; it is an agile animal, attacking from the rear. It's astute and knows human beings. This is vicious. The animal isn't psychologically well."

This was undeniably very plausible. But, as is so often the case when people try and reconcile alleged chupacabra attacks in a down-to-earth fashion, there was a problem—the doors to the enclosure had not been forced open. There was nothing to indicate how the wolf, coyote, hybrid, or feral hound had entered the zoo and subsequently exited it too. And, taking into consideration the savage nature of the attacks, why, aside from those of the goats themselves, were no paw prints or hairs found at the site of the bloody mayhem? It's a question that left many to conclude that the chupacabra had expanded its hunting ground to right in the heart of Rio Piedras, an 18th century district of San Juan itself. Whether or not the culprit really was a chupacabra, that the incident should have occurred just as *Proof Positive* aired was uncanny.

Chapter 10

FIELDS FILLED WITH FEAR

A few months before 2005 came to a close, I was again Puerto Rico bound. And here's how it all began: Paul Kimball is a good friend of mine who hails from Halifax, Nova Scotia, Canada. He's an author and moviemaker, and the brains behind Red Star Films. His constant traveling companion is, rather disturbingly, a stuffed toy known as Admiral Zorgrot. He (that's Paul, not the admiral) likes jangly shit, such as the Smiths and REM. And free-form jazz, too. But I don't hold that against him. At least, I try not to. Paul's also a man who loves a good mystery, which brings me to the next aspect of the story.

The so-called cattle mutilation enigma has long plagued the United States, Canada, and numerous other countries. Animals are found slain, missing vital organs, blood, and sometimes even limbs. Strange lights are seen in the skies. Black helicopters hover over the dead cows. For some researchers, cattle mutations are the work of deadly extraterrestrials, who are engaged in deranged, genetic experimentation, the likes of which would have made even Dr. Victor Frankenstein shiver. Other investigators point their accusing fingers in the direction of military programs revolving around secret, biological warfare operations. The most disturbing theory, however, is that the mutilators originate deep within government agencies. Their alleged task is to secretly monitor the cattle herds of numerous nations because nightmarish and near-unstoppable viruses have entered the food chain and pose a potentially fatal threat to anyone and everyone with a love of red meat.

Although Paul was, and still is, highly skeptical of the idea that cattle mutilations are the work of anything but natural predators, he felt that a comprehensive television documentary on the subject might be ideal for Canada's Space Channel, which in style and content is very much like the SyFy Channel in the United States. So Paul did some research, put a proposal together, and pitched it to the channel. They loved it. As a direct result, wheels were soon in motion, as was a trip to Puerto Rico, when Paul asked me if I would like to come along on the investigation and filming.

Searching for Vampires—Again

Darkness had already fallen upon the island when my plane began its smooth descent into Luis Munoz Marin International Airport. As I looked out the window of the 737, the bright lights of San Juan loomed into view, flickering like fireflies, and beckoning invitingly and warmly. Thirty minutes or so after touchdown, I had cleared security, picked up my suitcase, and was sitting in a van with Paul, his brother Jim, and the cameraman and the sound guy, John Rosborough and Findlay Muir. I had met Jim and John on previous shoots. Findlay, I didn't know, but was pleased to find that he originally hailed from Scotland, home, of course, to yet another famous monster, Nessie. As Paul told me, while Jim drove us to our hotel, we had a hectic week ahead of us, one destined to be packed with a wide and varied body of cases, locations, and interviewees.

After a shower, dinner, and a few drinks with the guys, I headed back to my room and grabbed a few hours of much needed shut-eye. As anyone who has ever pursued a monster will tell you, being alert, wide awake, and ready for action is the name of the game. I slept like the proverbial log.

On the Occult Road

I was jolted awake by my alarm clock at around 8:00 a.m. Within an hour, we were all revved up and ready to go. I have to say that some of the most fascinating revelations surfaced not in the field, but in the confines of the van. Since we typically had thirty or more minutes of driving between locations, it gave all of us the opportunity to hang out, chat, and share stories. Our Puerto Rican guide, Orlando, was a veritable mine of information.

I wasn't sure if Orlando was a full-on believer in the creature, a middle of the road skeptic, or a downright debunker. It turned out, very refreshingly, that he was none of those. Instead, he had a totally open and unbiased approach to the controversy. Very interestingly, he took the view that the phenomenon of the chupacabra was actually a combination of multiple phenomena. All of which had become fused into one unholy thing: the goat sucker. And downright confusingly fused, too, I should stress.

Orlando explained, specifically for the camera, that trying to suggest or to theorize that the chupacabra was this or was that was completely pointless. The trick to solving the riddle was to take each case on its own merit. Some cases of animal mutilation, he said, were absolutely nothing to do with the chupacabra, but were the work of occultists who had an agenda that involved the exploitation of the vampire stories. He told of an investigation that had been run out of the FBI's field office in Puerto Rico, which is situated on Carlos Chardon Avenue in the Hato Rey region of San Juan. It was in the 1990s when Bureau agents got caught up in an investigation that revolved around nothing less than the world of voodoo.

In various parts of the island, the bodies of numerous animals were turning up dead, all bearing the classic marks of vampirism: savage attacks to the neck and a profound lack of blood. But there was something very odd about the killings. The necks of the animals had been shaved clean; where the blood had been removed, not a single hair was in sight. What were the chances that the monster had an aversion to hair and had carefully removed each and every follicle by means unknown? Zero, that's what the chances were!

It turned out that the culprits were occultists who followed a particularly dark offshoot of voodoo and who used animal blood in their rites. The marks to the necks were not bites. Shaving the hair on the relevant part of the neck simply made matters easier for the guilty parties to get the job done. To cover their tracks, however, and in the specific regions where the killings occurred, the group deliberately spread tales of the chupacabra and its penchant for blood.

Born To Be Wild

There was a significant likelihood that some of the attacks that had been attributed to chupacabras were really the savage work of wild dogs, Orlando commented for the camera. Certainly, the island is not short of them. In fact, they are everywhere.

Whether singly, in pairs, or even in packs of seven or eight, wild dogs are a staple part of life in Puerto Rico. They're particularly prevalent in the smaller towns and villages, as well as in the poorer parts of Old San Juan. You cannot fail to see them, scowling and prowling their way around the streets, scavenging for food, fighting with each other for top position, and generally doing their best to look menacing. They do a damned good job of it too.

The theory that some chupacabra killings had down-to-earth explanations was one supported by a notable individual, Wisbel Alaya, who held a senior position in Puerto Rico's civil defense department. When, in 1996, a pair of sheep was found slaughtered on a Lajas farm, Alaya looked into the killings, suggesting they were the work of monkeys living in the area.

They must have been pretty aggressive monkeys, I thought, to have successfully brought down and snuffed the life out of two fully grown sheep. Alaya was also at the forefront of another investigation, this one into the death of a turkey that belonged to a man who lived in Mayaguez. The death of this animal, too—found with deep claw marks on its neck—was said to have been caused by a rogue monkey.

By 2005, however, when Paul Kimball and I turned up at Alaya's compact, red and white brick offices in a small, out of the way town, his views were somewhat different. It was dogs, and not monkeys, that were now on Alaya's mind.

Doggedly Pursuing the Answers

Alaya was a friendly, affable guy and someone who was very open to talking for the camera. Paul and the crew set up the equipment and focused the camera on Alaya, who got straight to the point. His investigations, back in the 1990s, were undertaken with a determined dedication to solving the mystery. As the camera continued to roll, Alaya said to the Red Star Films team he was sure he and his colleagues had done exactly that. In many cases, provisions were made available for the careful collection of body parts, blood, and skin from the slain animals, all of which were studiously preserved, then examined and analyzed by experts in the field of forensics. The conclusion was that wild dogs carried out the vast majority of the attacks. For Alaya, it was a perfectly normal and natural aspect of life in Puerto Rico, but an aspect that hysteria, fear mongering, and media sensationalism had transformed into something quite different.

In 2014, Ken Gerhard, a good friend and chupacabra authority, told me that he too felt some Puerto Rico–based attacks attributed to the chupacabra were very likely the work of hungry, savage hounds. He said, "In Puerto Rico, in many of the initial livestock killings, the culprits may have been wild dogs. Perhaps, with the people of Puerto Rico being so rooted in folklore, people jumped to the conclusion that chupacabras were responsible."

Opening Up the Vampire Files

To demonstrate that not everyone who worked in the field of civil defense was of the opinion that wild dogs were behind the chupacabra legend, the next day we met with a retired employee of the agency, a man who now faithfully tended a place called the Town of the Stones. It was an amazing, mini-Stonehenge style creation situated deep within enchanting, magical woods. For me, this was the highlight of the week.

Visiting the Town of Stones.

Admiral Zorgrot was carefully placed on a nearby fence-post, and a camera started to run and hum. As we chatted, the man revealed that when he left the department, he took something with him. It was something fascinating, something astounding. One would be wholly justified in calling it a real-life "X-file." He described it as a huge, thick, official dossier. It dated from the 1990s and was filled with reports, drawings, witness accounts, newspaper and magazine articles, and photographs, all relative to the chupacabra. I asked him if I could take a look at it. He smiled in return. That was a good sign!

The man walked over to his truck and put his hand through the open passenger-side window. He pulled a large file from the passenger seat and walked back to me. He handed me the file and I enthusiastically opened it. I studied its contents carefully. They contained no references to wild dogs, but were overflowing with data on the goat sucker. There were detailed pieces of artwork showing the spiky heads and backs of the beasts. Color pictures, taken by civil defense staff, graphically showed farm animals said to have been torn apart by one or more chupaca-bra. There was an abundance of autopsy reports. The official crest of the civil defense agency could be seen on dozens of pages. I asked the man what he thought the chupacabra might be. He replied that he had no idea what it was. But he knew that it wasn't a wild dog.

Admiral Zorgrot and Paul Kimball, fearless vampire hunters!

Chapter 11

A DEADLY PREDATOR CALLS

As the days progressed, so did our investigations. I said in the previous chapter that my encounter with the man with the file was the highlight of the week. It was. A close second, however, was an interview with a farmer who lived in a small, isolated village, pretty much in the middle of nowhere. Late one night, approximately five years earlier, he jumped out of bed to the screams of his pigs; he was a breeder and seller of the animals. And, given that this was his only source of income, he raced to the back door, grabbed a machete and a flashlight, flung the door open, and charged out into the muggy darkness. The scene was one of carnage.

The bodies of a number of dead, blood-splattered rabbits, which the farmer also kept, were strewn about the yard, many torn to pieces. And one of his prize pigs was dead too, lying on the ground. All of them, the pig and the rabbits, were killed in the same fashion, via three huge puncture wounds to the neck. As the man, pretty much in a state of shock, prowled around the tree-shrouded yard, he heard movement in the undergrowth. Wasting no time at all, he threw the machete in what he thought was the right direction. His instinct was right; the machete slammed into something solid. The sound was akin to metal hitting metal. Whatever it was, it didn't hang around. In seconds, it was gone, having leapt into the safety of the all-encompassing, nearby woods. There were even weirder developments to come, in the form of none other than the dreaded Men in Black. Or, to be completely accurate—a man and a woman in black.

Not Will Smith and Tommy Lee Jones

It was early the next morning when the darkly garbed duo descended upon the man's farm. They asked all sorts of questions about the previous night's events, making it clear to him that they knew far more about the attack in particular, and the mysterious attacker in general, than they were willing to admit. The strange pair listened in an emotionless fashion to everything that he had to say, then suddenly turned on their heels and vanished into the woods, along with his machete, which they made clear they were confiscating. Maybe wisely, he decided not to object. He never saw them or his machete ever again. Nor, to his relief, did he ever encounter that mysterious, midnight predator, either.

Then there was the story of a huge flying bird.

A Flying Mutilator

Our source, the resident of a small village that was home to a cool-looking church, one which rather reminded me of an old English castle, had an encounter in early 2005 with…well… something. It clearly wasn't your average chupacabra, but it did end with multiple animal mutilations, so, in that sense, the story has relevance. The month, the man thought, was February, and the time definitely late evening. He was walking past the old church when an ear-splitting roar filled the air. It came from an area dominated by tall, thick trees and barely fifty feet away. Frozen rigid in his tracks, he stared intently at the woods.

The site of an encounter with a winged monster.

Suddenly, something terrifying happened. A huge, feathery beast burst through the trees and took to the skies. Whatever the creature was, it was no ordinary bird; the incredible size of it, somewhere in the region of a man, made that abundantly clear. The man could only stare in awe as the infernal thing flapped its mighty wings and vanished into the distance.

Okay, granted, it didn't sound like the chupacabra, but I make mention of the case because our witness pointed out that only a couple of days later, and at a very nearby farm, numerous animals were violently slain by an unknown predator. Was this case an indication that Puerto Rico was home to something even more terrible than the chupacabra? Could there have been a connection to the winged beast that Anna had encountered back in 1975? These were questions that, near inevitably, remained unresolved.

Still on the matter of additional oddities on the island, I heard a few stories of sightings of giant reptiles in Puerto Rico. They reportedly looked suspiciously like velociraptors, those savage beasts that roamed around in the latter part of the Cretaceous period, seventy-five million years ago. More correctly, the creatures sounded like the raptors as they were specifically portrayed in *Jurassic Park*. The reality is that the real velociraptors were much smaller than in the movies and they sported feathers. It's a testament to the movie's success, however, that the public's image of the velociraptor is that created by Hollywood, rather than by nature. Far more like the raptors of the movies was Deinonychus, an eleven-foot-long, clawed, killing machine that lived around one hundred and ten million years ago, but not in Puerto Rico, I should stress. I had no way to explain what had been seen. Today, I still don't.

Part 2

THE GOAT SUCKER IN THE UNITED STATES AND MEXICO

Chapter 12

THE ELMENDORF BEAST

It's notable that plans for my July 2004 expedition to Puerto Rico began in April of that year. You might justifiably ask, why so? Well, I'll tell you. This was the very same period in which the chupacabra mystery came to the heart of the United States. Or, to be absolutely precise, to my home state of Texas. That's right, while Jon Downes and I were racing around the wilds of Puerto Rico, dark and foul things were afoot in the Texas town of Elmendorf. Around seventeen miles outside of the city of San Antonio, a chupacabra reared its ugly head. Unlike the sprawling city, which is famous for being the home of the legendary Alamo, Elmendorf is small in the extreme. It is currently home to no more than one thousand, five hundred people and is less than five square miles in size. For such a tiny and obscure locale, unbridled, near-worldwide infamy was waiting just around the corner.

There was something very unusual about the chupacabra of Elmendorf. The famous moniker aside, it was acutely different, in terms of its physical appearance, from the Puerto Rican original. The creature of the island, as you will have come to appreciate, was bipedal in nature and had a vicious-looking row of spikes running along the back of its head, as well as down the length of its neck and spine. Some people, as you will also now know, even reported that the creature was bat-winged and possessed a pair of bright, glowing red eyes. All of this, and I do mean all of this, was in sharp contrast to the description of the animal that first became known as the Elmendorf Beast, and then and forever, the Texas chupacabra.

Initial photographs, coupled with Internet chatter and gossip, suggested that an oversized, hairless, rat-like animal was the cause of what turned out to be a few weeks' worth of terror and mayhem in and around Elmendorf. Careful evaluation of the evidence, however, revealed that the creature was not a giant, bald rodent after all, but something else entirely. What the enigmatic thing really was, and how it became saddled with the name of the Texas chupacabra, is a very strange story, one that I followed carefully from day one.

A Small Town Becomes Infamous

Devin McAnally, the owner of an Elmendorf ranch, lost somewhere in the region of fifty chickens to an unknown predator in the early months of 2004. He found himself falling victim to a beast of lethal proportions, always under cover of an overwhelming blanket of darkness. It began with the killing of five of his chickens, then twelve, and then in excess of thirty, and…well, you get the picture and the progression. There was something downright odd going on, though I knew that much from the intense media coverage that was occurring. Local newspapers, radio, television, and numerous Internet sites were reporting on just about every aspect of the affair. Soon the national press was commenting and observing on the controversy. It was big news everywhere and was enthusiastically lapped up like a chupacabra lapping blood. The collective story the media told went like this:

Whatever had killed the chickens made no attempts to devour them. The bodies of the birds were left where they fell, completely untouched, aside from wounds to the neck. Could McAnally's very own dog have been the culprit? No, it was not. Although, it must be said, his dog did play a role in the affair, an absolutely integral role, as it transpires. It was the barking of his dog on what turned out to be a fateful day indeed that finally revealed the beast to McAnally. And what a beast it was.

Racing along the fields was an odd, canid-looking animal. The first thought was that it was a greyhound gone wild. At first glance, at least, this was actually not entirely impossible, since a trio of greyhounds had been dumped in the area sometime earlier. The dog theory quickly became less and less likely: the creature ran in a very strange fashion and its coat appeared to be of a slight blue color. There was something else too. The presence of both McAnally and his dog seemed to have no effect on the beast. It was apparently fearless about their presence. This, most certainly, was not the typical behavior of the average coyote.

Twice more, and in fairly quick progression, the animal appeared on the ranch. There was just one problem, as on both occasions McAnally's rifle was inside his ranch house. McAnally raced to get his weapon, but the creature was gone by the time he returned to the fields. Then McAnally had a brainstorm. Next time he was going to be one hundred percent ready. Preparation was the name of the game; he positioned his loaded .22 rifle in a tree fork and patiently waited for the day when the animal returned. As fate would decree, he did not have to wait long at all.

Although the animal had developed a reputation born of both hostility and savagery, its downfall came when it was doing nothing more unusual than feeding on the fruit of a mulberry tree. Certainly not something that the average, self-respecting vampire would ever want to be caught doing! McAnally, who was carrying a couple of buckets of water at the time, knew that this was the time to strike. He carefully and quietly placed the buckets on the ground and made his way stealthily towards the animal. It was a testament to McAnally's hunting skills that the creature never even knew what hit it. One shot felled the beast in an instant.

McAnally walked over to it and was both shocked and puzzled by the horrific sight before him. The thing was hardly muscular. In fact, it was probably barely twenty pounds in weight and was hairless, aside from what appeared to be a slight mane that extended along its back. It was the skin that was strangest of all, however; it really was of a bluish color. Vicious-looking teeth, far bigger than those of a coyote, dominated the mouth of the beast. Its tail looked like that of some monstrous, goliath-sized rodent. The limbs did not appear to be of normal proportions. It was, then, a definitive enigma. Somewhat concerned by the nature of the animal, McAnally was reluctant to touch it. And who can blame him? So he did something else instead; he pumped two more bullets into its body. You know, just in case.

Although McAnally showed the corpse to a number of his neighbors, none of them could offer any kind of explanation for what the animal was. Baffled, he decided to bury the body in red clay, which can help to extend the preservation process, in the event that he might want to dig it up at a later date. Before doing so, however, McAnally took a couple of photos of the creature.

It wasn't long before they reached the Internet, and my eyes, and the phenomenon of the Texas chupacabra was brought to life in spectacular fashion.

As to why a hairless, four-legged freak in Texas became part of the chupacabra phenomenon, our attentions have to turn to the work of a good friend of mine: Ken Gerhard.

The Chupacabra: A Coyote?

I first met Ken, the vocalist with the band Bozo Porno Circus and a greatly respected cryptozoologist, in 2003, at the Texas-based Southern Crypto Conference, which was held in the town of Conroe. It quickly became apparent that we shared several mutual passions: loud music, wild adventure, road trips, and monsters. In the more than a decade since we first hung out, Ken and I have pursued supernatural goatmen in Texas, Bigfoot in Oklahoma, and the chupacabra (of course!). Ken also had the good fortune to spend time with McAnally and was able to dig deep in the strange, burgeoning mystery of the Texas goat sucker.

As for his assessment of McAnally, Ken, a resident of San Antonio, Texas, said in the pages of his *Monsters of Texas* book:

> My first thought was that Devin reminded me of the
> stereotypical Texan from a John Wayne movie: lean
> and muscular with a distinct drawl and skin that's been
> hardened by years of working in the hot Lone Star
> State sun. Devin has descended from a long line of
> McAnallys in Texas, having been born and raised in the
> Panhandle, along with four siblings, and taught to be
> self-sufficient by his father, a Methodist minister. What
> I didn't realize was that Devin has a master's degree

and has studied abroad, working as a bilingual English teacher for over forty years in the Texas school systems. Consequently, the man possesses a keen intellect and a truly vast knowledge of Tex-Mex history and culture. He had simply decided over the course of his life that he was happiest working outdoors and raising his chickens, which he has done on his property near Elmendorf for nearly two decades.

When we chatted about all things vampiric, I asked Ken, "When did you first hear the term 'chupacabra' used in relation to these animals in Texas?"

Ken got straight to the point. "This was with the Elmendorf Beast. It occurred shortly after the animal was discovered and the pictures were posted on the Internet. I found, through the course of my research, that what happened with the name change from Elmendorf Beast to chupacabra is that in an attempt to find out the identity of this creature, pictures were posted up at a local market near Elmendorf. This was a market where many old-timers went. Some of the older Mexican-American people that went into the market saw the photos and began referring to it as a chupacabra. And that's how the name started here in Texas."

Others, Ken told me, thought the creature of Elmendorf might have been a Xolo—a hairless Mexican dog. The theory that it was a small Muntjac deer was also offered as a suggestion, although, admittedly, it was a highly unlikely one. Neither suggestion took hold quite like the chupacabra one, however, which should not be surprising to anyone. Even the experts were baffled. Indeed, when the San Antonio Zoo got their hands on the skull of the beast of Elmendorf, not a single, solitary member of staff could make a definitive identification. Maybe it was a coyote with mange, a condition that is caused by a mite and which can cause massive hair loss, as well as intense irritation, infection, and death. Possibly it was a wolf-coyote cross. Perhaps it was a coyote-dog hybrid. This latter suggestion was made to the press by the zoo's staff. Nevertheless, even they couldn't fail to note something unusual, as Ken pointed out. "The skull possessed a very poor fusion in the jaw area, which seemed to allow its jaw to spread in an abnormal way, appearing more akin to the jaw of a reptile than that of a mammal."

Whatever the actual answer to the mystery, it was clear that as the weeks and months progressed, the coyote theory was becoming more and more popular and accepted. Eventually, DNA analysis proved the coyote suspicions to be correct. As for the hair loss—nothing but severe mange, suggested the experts. But is that all there really was, and still is, to the Texas chupacabra? That's an important question to which we'll come back later. First, however, let's see what happened next, chronologically speaking, in the saga of the chupacabra of the Lone Star State.

Jon Downes Gets In on the Act

Considering the speed with which the images of the Elmendorf Beast went viral, it wasn't long before the world of television sat up and took keen notice. It was a development that brought my old mate Jon Downes back into the picture.

By mid- to late 2004, interest in the phenomenon of the Texas chupacabra had reached near-hysteria, to the extent that Jon was invited over to the Lone Star State to film a show on the infamous creature, for the Discovery Channel, no less. Given that this was only months after Jon and I had undertaken a weeklong trek around Puerto Rico in search of the original chupacabra, Jon kept me fully informed of the intricacies of the investigation, which was undertaken with his then-girlfriend.

Having reviewed the available evidence in hand, Jon was far from convinced that the entire mystery could be explained away by nothing stranger than mange. In fact, Jon's controversial conclusion was at the absolute other end of the spectrum. In his book, *The Island of Paradise*, Jon commented as follows:

> We came here looking for the corpse of a chupacabra. Not surprisingly, we found no such thing. What we have here is something far more exciting. There is a great misconception in cryptozoology that all unknown species are prehistoric survivors. What people forget is that evolution is a continuum. What we have here might be an example of evolution in action. We might be seeing the beginnings of a new species evolving away from the coyote species as a result of the environmental pressures of life at the beginning of the twenty-first century.

As we'll see later, Jon's conclusions just may be right on target. Let's now take a look at what happened, in relation to the Texas chupacabra controversy, post-Elmendorf.

There's Something Under the House

I heard a few intriguing, but unsubstantiated, stories of other encounters with chupacabras in and around the Dallas area in late 2004, all of them of the canid and hairless variety, and none of them of the bipedal, spiky variety. The next case of real significance, however, surfaced in October 2004, out of Pollok,

Texas, a tiny town a little more than ten miles from the city of Lufkin, which is dominated by the one hundred and twenty mile long Lufkin River. It was a case that the *Lufkin Daily News* was quickly on top of, possibly even faster than a chupacabra on a goat.

The focus of all the action, the press revealed over the course of a number of articles, was the home of the O'Quinn family. It would have been a normal day for the O'Quinns had something profoundly strange not spooked their dogs. But, as fate would have it, that's exactly what happened. Whatever the creature was, with the hounds on its tail it raced for the safety of the small crawl space between the base of the house and the dusty ground below. Rather interestingly, despite having the creature cornered and surrounded, none of the significantly sized dogs was willing to take it on in a head-to-head fight. Not that we should blame them for that. It was left up to Tyrel O'Quinn to crawl under the building and see what was causing all the calamitous commotion. He very quickly found it.

Tyrel was confronted by something downright terrifying: a dog-sized, hairless rat, one with exaggerated claws and savage-looking fangs. Rather, that's what it looked like. Attempts to pull the creature out with ropes failed. There was only option left. Tyrel's father, Ben, shot it dead.

As luck would have it, a relative of the O'Quinns', named Stacy Womack, worked at a nearby veterinary clinic. With the weird situation explained to her, she drove out to see the remains of the creature. Incredibly, as she got near the O'Quinns' home, Womack saw a near-identical beast cross the road right in front of her. Was it perhaps the mate of the dead animal? That's exactly what Womack thought.

Womack's study of the creature revealed a number of interesting things, including the fact that the front legs of the shot animal were far shorter than its back legs, its skin was bluish, and those huge teeth were just plain wrong. Once again, there was a lack of solid consensus on what the creature was, even within regular zoological circles. When the *Lufkin Daily News* highlighted Womack's photo of the dead animal, a deformed coyote was suggested, as was a fox with mange. And what of its mate: was that just an identically deformed coyote too? The questions were many. The answers, unfortunately, were not. The controversy of the Texas chupacabra was brewing very nicely.

Chapter 13

THE YEAR OF THE CHUPACABRA

August 2007 was the month that, in the minds and eyes of many (including me), the phenomenon of the Texas chupacabra really came of age. It was all thanks to a woman named Phylis Canion, a doctor of nutrition. As with so many other chupacabra cases, whether in Puerto Rico or Texas, the affair began when Canion noticed that animals were going missing from her property, which was in the Texas town of Cuero. Kittens were the first things to vanish. Chickens were soon found lying dead around the Canion home reportedly missing significant amounts of blood. As was the case with the Elmendorf creature in 2004, both the Texas-based and national media were hot on the trail and reported on the mystery extensively.

At first, it appeared there was a rational explanation for the events. A bobcat was seen in the area, one which was eventually fatally shot. Unfortunately, the killings of the animals did not stop. It wasn't long before Canion, along with her husband, Steve, caught sight of the real culprit. It was a beast whose appearance baffled both of them. This was surprising to the pair, as they had spent years living in Africa, encountering and hunting all manner of wild and exotic animals. They had clearly, however, not seen everything. The animal that was causing all the mayhem was coyote-like, but lacked the typical attributes of the creature. Unlike nearby coyotes, this one was not in the slightest bit bothered by the presence of people in its midst, and it appeared to hunt during the day, rather than under a blanket of darkness.

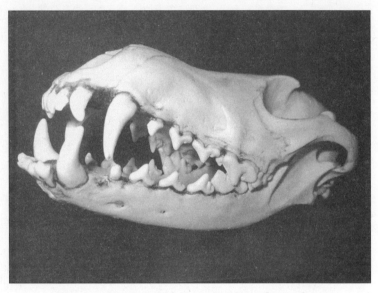

Terror across Texas: The Lone Star State chupacabra.

Puzzled, and more than a bit concerned by the presence of the creature and its attacks on her very own animals, Phylis contacted some of her neighbors to see if they too had seen the elusive, mysterious thing. It transpires that, yes, they had seen it. But sightings of the creature were nothing compared to the next development in the story. After she got the word out about what was going down around town, Phylis had a call from a local person who informed her there was a very odd-looking animal lying dead on the road, not at all far from the Canion ranch. Phylis wasted no time hauling ass, as they say in Texas, and checking out the peculiar piece of road-kill for herself. She did not just examine the dead animal, however—she also brought its remains home. It was then that Phylis was able to make a careful study of the beast that had so fortuitously fallen into her lap.

Like so many other Texas chupacabras, this one was lacking in hair, aside from a very thin line of hair along its spine. Its teeth, just like those of the Elmendorf Beast, were extremely long. There were discrepancies in the lengths of the limbs; the hind legs were far longer than would normally be expected in a canid of the coyote type. It was packing some considerable muscle too. Whereas so many of the other creatures given the name Texas chupacabra were emaciated and small, this one was anything but. It looked well fed, healthy, and definitely not something to be messed with. Canion quickly took photos of the animal, thus forever preserving the strangeness that lay stretched out before her.

Less than a week later, two more near-identical animals turned up dead in the area. While it was odd that a trio of such animals should have surfaced in a short period of time, Canion had a theory to explain this. At the time, there was significant flooding in the nearby creeks, something that led Canion to suggest the turbulent waters had caused the animals to flee the area. Forced to leave their regular hunting and sleeping grounds behind them, they edged closer to the heart of civilization, which ultimately proved to be their downfall.

The strange nature of the animals, the alleged blood draining of the chickens, and the missing kittens led Canion to believe that what she had in her possession was, yes, a chupacabra.

Considering the body to be a significant find, she removed its head and skin, and preserved its flesh in a freezer. She also became quite enterprising and had T-shirts printed that read "2007 The Year of the Chupacabra." They sold not in the dozens or hundreds, but in the thousands. Cuero and its people became the focal point for monster hunting.

"Why Does this Coyote Look so Un-coyote-like?"

As far as the scientific community was concerned, the matter of Phylis Canion's chupacabra was resolved in late 2007. A sample of the DNA of the Cuero creature was provided to Joe Conger of KENS 5 news, who in turn passed it on to a man named John Baccus, the director of the Wildlife Ecology Program, based at Texas State University. Baccus gave the sample to Mike Forstner of the university's biology department. That was when the detective work began in earnest. DNA analysis of the chupacabra was virtually identical to that of a coyote.

Forstner told the media, "This is probably the answer a lot of folks thought might be the outcome. I myself really thought it was a domestic dog, but the Cuero chupacabra is a Texas coyote."

Although the DNA study provided the answer to what the creature was, Jayme Blaschke of the university news service made a valid point and asked an equally valid question: Why did the body of the creature look so much unlike a coyote? Mange was suggested, but the problem was that without a living specimen to examine, there was no way to be sure. And, of course, mange could not explain that very curious angle of the oddly sized limbs.

"It Was Pretty Hideous when Phylis
Pulled this Frozen Head out of the Freezer"

In 2008, the popular History Channel show *Monster Quest* got in on the vampire action. The producers of the show hired Ken Gerhard to investigate the matter of the Cuero chupacabra, to try and have the matter resolved once and for all and to the satisfaction of everyone. Also onboard was a friend of Ken's, a naturalist named Lee Hales. Before the production of the episode began, Ken paid a visit to the Canion home and was provided with a firsthand look at the remains of the beast that had provoked so much intrigue and so many T-shirt sales.

"It was pretty hideous when Phylis pulled this frozen head out of the freezer," Ken told me. He said it was "quite broad and square, not at all like the familiar streamlined head of a coyote." He confirmed the presence of the oversized fangs and the overall odd nature of the beast's physical form.

As for the *Monster Quest* shoot, it was Ken and Lee's role to try and encourage further potential chupacabras in the area to surface by enticing them with raw meat, which was carefully spread around the Canions' ranch. And, given the chupacabra's taste for chickens, a live one was placed in a cage in the hope that it might provoke one of the hairless oddities to seek it out for food. Next to the cage was a steel trap into which, it was earnestly hoped, a hungry chupacabra just might walk and become snared. Just for good measure, Ken had the unenviable task of spraying the surrounding area with coyote urine; such are the unenviable trials and tribulations of those of us that have a fascination with monsters!

There then followed a nighttime vigil, in which dogs, wild or otherwise, were heard nearby. Unfortunately, however, nothing of any substance occurred. The meat was evidently not the kind preferred by a discerning chupacabra, the trap caught nothing but a possum, and the chicken was relieved to have lived to tell the tale, so to speak. *Monster Quest* was not quite done yet, however.

The show's producers decided to have their own experts study the DNA of Phylis Canion's terrifying trophy. The results were not unexpected, although they differed slightly from the conclusions of staff at Texas State University. *Monster Quest's* experts suggested the Cuero animal was part-coyote and part-wolf.

"I Don't Want to Annihilate Them"

One year later, Jon Downes had the opportunity to study, in person, Phylis Canion's by now stuffed and mounted chupacabra. Jon said of the animal that it displayed monorchism (it had only one testicle, rather than two) and its eyes were a "remarkable pale blue."

Jon, in an article specifically commissioned by *Fortean Times* magazine, commented as follows on the eye color: "I would have taken exception to this, and assumed that it was the result of incompetent taxidermy, but Dr. Canion showed me a photograph which proved that this was exactly the same as the eye color."

There was something else of deep significance too, as Jon observed. The creature, he said, "was mounted in a peculiar hunch-backed position. I asked Dr. Canion about this, and she confirmed that when she has seen the specimens of these animals alive, they have stood in this very manner."

Jon noted other anomalies too. The Cuero creature only had three phalanges, or toes, on each of its front paws, instead of the customary four, which was really weird. It had only four teats, instead of the usual eight or ten—equally odd. Jon also observed that the creature displayed a pair of what appeared to be large pouches on its hindquarters. Jon was of the opinion that the pouches were actually anal glands, possibly highly infected when the creature lived, and, as a result, still enlarged at the time of its death. Canion, on the other hand, was sure this was not the case. She said of the so-called pouches that, "I cut into one for a DNA test and there was nothing but solid red meat."

The final word (so far) on the Cuero chupacabra goes to Phylis Canion. Although she is devoted to securing more DNA examples, something that might allow for some of the physical anomalies to be resolved, Canion told the *Huffington Post*: "I don't want to annihilate them."

Chapter 14

THE MONSTER INVADES
MEXICO AND MY MAILBOX

In June 2008, I flew to Monterrey, Mexico, for just one day. Yet again, the domain of television was paying my way to investigate what I was told was a chupacabra attack. It turned out that back in 2006, a large number of lambs had been killed on a farm somewhere on the fringes of Cadereyta Jimenez, Nuevo Leon, Mexico, which dates back to the seventeenth century. There were the usual stories of savage mutilations and drained blood. This time, however, there was something significantly different: the presence of a large, beaked, winged monster that was presumed to have been the culprit behind all the bloody carnage. The word was it was a chupacabra, even though to me it hardly sounded like one. The production company knew the case was valid because they had found a story about it on the Internet, as if that somehow legitimized it with one hundred percent certainty. In light of all this, I assumed that I would be on-site to interview the farmer, check out the scene, and offer my thoughts. Not so. Things turned out to be very different. Try as they might, the team couldn't find the ranch at all. So it was time for a bit of improvisation.

Making the Best of a Bad Situation

We drove out to a suitably appropriate place for the filming. It was an old, run-down, and clearly long-abandoned building about fifteen miles outside of the city, in a definitive desert setting. The crew set up the equipment and the main researcher outlined what my role was to be. I would pretend that this was the real ranch where the attacks occurred. I would pretend that I had spoken with the rancher. And I would pretend that I had examined the dead lambs, although not a single thought was apparently given to why the farmer might still possess the rotted remains of his animals a full one-and-a-half years after they were killed, no less!

As the researcher continued to tell me what I was to do, I interrupted with words that, working from memory, went very much like this: "I'm not pretending anything. I don't lie for the cameras. I'm not saying anything about this being the right farm, I haven't interviewed anyone, and where is the lamb?"

The researcher then had the complete and utter nerve to tell me this was reality television and, for that reason, no one would ever know or even care. Well, I knew and I definitely cared! She even tried her very best to make me feel guilty by inferring that the shoot was now in jeopardy and it was all my fault! That was when the proverbial you-know-what hit the proverbial fan. The only thing I was prepared to do, I said, was to talk about the chupacabra in generalities: the history of the phenomenon, the alleged mode of attack and killing, the blood-draining allegations, and so on. It was that, and that alone, or nothing at all. The woman grudgingly agreed to my terms. So, for the next two hours or thereabouts, I spoke before the camera on the subjects of my treks around Puerto Rico and Texas, and my thoughts on the nature of the beast.

That was not all; they had actually brought with them a silver cross, a wooden stake, and even a bag containing cloves of garlic! Would I be willing to talk about how those particular items had become ingrained into vampire lore? Well, that was not a problem. I was, however, very careful to point out that while a carefully sharpened stake would obviously take out a chupacabra, in just the same way that it might take out any animal, garlic and silver were unlikely to have any effect whatsoever.

The researcher asking the questions wasn't happy. Couldn't I be a bit ambiguous on the garlic and silver angle, and leave the controversy a tad open? No, I could not leave things a tad open, nor was I prepared to be a bit ambiguous. Garlic and silver are fine for television, movies, and novels, but not in the real world. The woman actually pouted at that. It was not, I should stress, a sensual, sexy pout, but a "screw you" pout. I thought: well, screw you, too!

There was, however, one bit of good news in this ridiculous escapade. The team had tracked down someone who lived high in the mountains outside of Monterrey and who had a sighting of a huge, winged beast back in 2007. Finally, a bit of light was on the horizon.

Flying Reptile
versus Infamous Blood-Drainer

The witness was a woman named Sofia, a vivacious, dark-haired woman of about thirty-five. I never did learn how the team had found her. I briefly pondered on the possibility that Sofia had been hauled from the streets of Monterrey and offered a wad of cash, all in exchange for telling a story that was plucked straight out of thin air. With time running out, and a catalog of disasters growing larger by the minute, the team just might have been that desperate. As the interview progressed, however, high in the mountains that surround Monterrey, I quickly found myself taking Sofia's story very seriously.

As I spoke with Sofia, she told me that the huge Cerro de las Mitras mountain overlooked the part of Monterrey in which she lived. As a hiker, Sofia loved to spend time walking its slopes. She said, too, that there had been a number of disappearances of both farm animals and pets in the area. This was more like it.

No corpses were ever located, no body parts were found strewn around the neighborhood, and there were no telltale pools of blood anywhere. The animals, which included cats, chickens, and goats, were simply gone. Sofia, however, believed she knew what was behind the attacks. It was a belief born out of something remarkable: she had seen the beast that she suspected was responsible for the disappearances.

On one particular Saturday morning, and at the height of the attacks, Sofia said, she was walking around the lower parts of Cerro de las Mitras when she briefly saw something abominable in the sky—a large, leathery-looking creature that appeared to be part bat and part bird. It was in view for a minute or so, gliding at a distance of around three or four hundred feet, before soaring away to the higher levels of the mountain. To me, it sounded very much like a classic description of a presumed long-extinct pterosaur, a flying reptile that lived from the

Triassic to the Cretaceous period and died out around sixty-six million years ago. It's a controversial fact, however, that Mexico, and particularly the region of the Texas-Mexico border, has been a hotbed for sightings of such creatures for decades. And it continues to be a hotbed too.

Pterosaur Terror

This is not the place for me to expand at length on the long and controversial history of Mexican pterosaur encounters. I did wonder, however—and I still wonder—if such creatures might still exist, against all the odds, in some of the larger mountains of Mexico. I also wondered, if they were still with us, was it possible that some of them were responsible for the attacks attributed to the chupacabra? After all, I had uncovered more than a few reports of the Puerto Rican chupacabra possessing large and leathery wings, not at all unlike those of a pterosaur. Some might say that suggesting the Puerto Rican chupacabra is a pterosaur is just plain outrageous. But I'm not alone in postulating such a controversial theory. Researcher David Hatcher Childress asked:

> Could the sudden rash of chupacabras attacks and sightings be related to the occasional rash of pteranodon sightings? Many of the aspects of the chupacabras and living pteranodons seem to match. They are both monsters and flesh eaters. Pteranodons may well drink blood and gorge themselves on internal organs, which are easy to eat.

Pterosaurs or chupacabras? Public domain: Edward Newman, 1843

Carrion birds such as vultures and condors eat the exposed softer flesh first, lips, eyes, underbelly, etc. It would seem natural for pteranodons to do this as well. Admittedly, the chupacabras' supposed habit of draining all the blood from two small holes on the neck, similar to the familiar vampires of lore, seems more fiction than reality.

In Chile, animals were actually disappearing or being half eaten. Pteranodons are vicious meat eaters with very sharp teeth and claws to rip open victims. They apparently feed at night, much like owls. Their survival in the mountains of northern Mexico and the southern Andes has been theorized for decades by cryptozoologists.

Goodbye and Good Riddance

By the time the interview with Sofia was concluded, it was coming up to 5:00 p.m. and my flight back to Dallas was scheduled for two-and-a-half hours later. My check was signed, the equipment was loaded into the van, Sofia waved goodbye and got into her car, and we all hit the road. The atmosphere in the van was frosty to the point of nearly being downright frozen solid. They knew they had screwed up and had failed to deliver the primary goods.

Over the years, I have appeared on roughly seventy television shows. Of that seventy or so, only specifically three failed to be broadcast. This was one of them. Despite Sofia's good, solid story, I was not surprised that the show never aired. I can't say I was particularly disappointed, either.

"It Looks Like It Ain't from Around Here"

Over the years, numerous photos and film footage have surfaced that purport to show chupacabras; most of it is nothing but fakery—and not particularly good fakery, I might add. But the most intriguing imagery, in my view, anyway, was that which surfaced in the aftermath of an August 2008 encounter in DeWitt County, Texas, just two months after I returned from Mexico.

It's hardly surprising that the imagery caught people's attention, and that of the nation's media, too, since it was taken by a police officer. There's no doubt that it showed a creature very much like that shot and killed by Devin McAnally in 2004, and that which fell into the hands of Phylis Canion three years later. There was, however, one thing about the DeWitt County chupacabra that really stood out prominently, and I do mean that literally, as you'll now come to appreciate.

As the sun was setting on the evening of August 8, Deputy Brandon Riedel was routinely patrolling the rural roads near Cuero with a trainee deputy when he got the shock of his life, as his onboard dash cam confirmed. While driving adjacent to a fence line on a dusty road, Riedel and his partner encountered something very strange. It was a hairless, four-legged animal racing ahead of them. Riedel quickly switched on the dash cam. They closed in on the animal, only to see something remarkable—the animal had a muzzle of epic proportions. Huge barely comes close. Ken Gerhard told me that it was very much like the snout of a pig. Ken was not wrong.

When the film hit the Internet (after it was first shown, and widely discussed, on CNN), I studied it extensively. As the animal bounds along the road, clearly aware it is being followed, it suddenly turns its head to the left. It's then that Riedel and his colleague get to see the head of the creature from a side perspective. To say that the muzzle dwarfs the rest of the head is not an understatement. It is massive. There was something else, too. Riedel, like so many other witnesses to such beasts, noted that there were significant discrepancies between the lengths of its front limbs and back limbs. In days, the footage and the attendant story surrounding it had gone viral. It remains one of the most fascinating pieces of film of what is purported to be a chupacabra.

Somewhat less well known was the encounter that occurred just a few weeks after Deputy Riedel's sighting and specifically in the nearby town of Terryville. It was August 30, when the next development in the saga of the DeWitt chupacabra surfaced. The location was the ranch of the grandfather of a man named Paul Jones, who was visiting with a few of his friends, Brian Wilborn, Cannon Simons, and Jason Marburger, to mow the fields in preparation for the upcoming deer season. All thoughts of deer, however, quickly evaporated when a certain strange beast appeared on the scene. It was quickly shot and killed by Jones. A few hours later, a second nearly identical animal was taken out of circulation by the guys. Jones mused on whether or not the dead animals could be chupacabras. Marburger was sure of one thing as he focused on the first slain beast: "I've seen pictures of coyotes. It doesn't look like any coyote or mixed breed I have ever seen. It looks like it ain't from around here," he told the press.

A Chupacabra Arrives in the Mail

November 2008 proved to be a turning point for me in pursuit of the Texas chupacabra. Since early 2008, I have lectured regularly in San Antonio, Texas, and specifically for the city's Mutual UFO Network (MUFON) group. One of the longest-running UFO study groups in the United States, MUFON was formed in 1969 by Texas native Walt Andrus. Even though Walt is now in his mid-nineties, he still regularly attends the San Antonio meetings. I was very pleased and surprised when, at the November meeting, Walt told me that he had then recently acquired the skull of a Texas chupacabra from a man who had killed it only weeks earlier after seeing it prowling around his property. I was even more pleased and surprised when Walt offered to let me have the skull. It was a gift I was hardly about to turn down!

Sure enough, it wasn't long before a carefully wrapped and boxed chupacabra skull appeared at my door, courtesy of FedEx, though I did wonder what the driver might have thought had he known he was carrying the bony remains of what some believe to be a blood-sucking, violent monster! No doubt the road would have been quickly sealed off and officials of the Centers for Disease Control, decked out in HAZMAT suits, would have descended upon my home.

The delivery was fortuitous, as shortly afterwards, the National Geographic Channel's *Paranatural* series was eager to film me with the skull, while I discussed my findings on the creature, both in Puerto Rico and Texas. *Paranatural* was particularly intrigued by the theory that the Puerto Rican chupacabras might actually be rhesus macaques, escaped from one or more research labs on the islands that make up Puerto Rico. In fact, that ultimately became the entire thrust of the interview. While I'm not convinced that this particular angle can explain away the whole mystery, I am of the opinion that it has almost certainly played at least some role in the way in which the controversy has progressed, as will later become apparent.

Chapter 15

GOAT SUCKERS ON THE MOVE

In September 2010, there was yet another development in my quest for the truth of the chupacabra in the United States, although this time not in Texas. It was a development that ultimately put a distinctly paranormal spin on at least certain aspects of the chupacabra phenomenon. That's far from how it all began, though. Matters kicked off with a phone call to me from Oklahoma's KOKH Fox 25 channel. It transpired that sightings had been made locally of what sounded very much like a Texas chupacabra, but over the border into Oklahoma. This account alone was of great interest to me, as it suggested the beast, or the condition that was provoking certain significant physical changes in wild coyotes, was on the move. There was more too.

Apparently, a photograph had been taken of the creature, one that showed it up close and personal. Not only that, at the time the photo was fortuitously snapped, the animal was in the process of bounding across a stretch of field in a very strange fashion: it alternated between running on all fours and almost bouncing along on its hind limbs. I had heard of accounts of the chupacabra (both in Puerto Rico and Texas) having the ability to move on both four limbs and two. This, however, was the first time I had come across a story where there was actual photographic evidence demonstrating this curious gait.

With the story outlined to me, a question was then put to me: "Would you like to come up and investigate the story with us?"

Hell, yes!

Barbecue to Beast

A couple of days later I was on the road. It was a blisteringly hot day in Texas when I set off. By the time I reached the town of Norman, Oklahoma, which was close to where all of the sightings had been made, it was roasting. The point of rendezvous was Rudy's Store and BBQ on Chautauqua Avenue. I was met by a Fox News reporter and a cameraman. As we ate our early dinner, and as the mouthwatering odor of barbecued meat filled the air, I was given the details of the story. For several months, sightings had been made of a strange creature, all at nearby Tecumseh, a small town of fewer than seven thousand people. What made this story particularly interesting is that the encounters were not strewn all across the town. Instead, each and every one was focused on the woods and the fields that surrounded the Tecumseh High School.

It was probably a coincidence (but given the dark and disturbing nature of the chupacabra phenomenon, it may not have been) that sightings of the animal began in May 2010. This was the very month that Tecumseh was pummeled by a violent hurricane, which caused major damage and destruction across town. Was it perhaps a precursor of the menace that was to follow? Based on all I had encountered in my quest for the truth of the monster, I didn't entirely rule out such a possibility.

I was told it was the very fact that the beast spent so much time in the area that allowed one of the school's students, Ryan Craighead, to get a picture of it on his cellphone. Fox News had a copy of the image with them and passed it to me for scrutiny. It did, indeed, show something very weird. Craighead had managed to photograph a creature that clearly resembled the animals in the possession of both Devin McAnally and Philis Canion. There were differences, however. They were major differences. Sure enough, the creature, as I had been told just a few days previously, appeared to be running on its hind legs. Not only that— the front limbs of the animal were ridiculously short. It was a very, very strange picture of a very, very strange animal.

The Quest for the
Bouncing Biped/Quadruped Begins

By about 5:30 p.m. we were on site, deep in the heart of the fields and woods that dominate the school. We did some background filming that outlined my investigations of the chupacabra controversy, and which also gave me time to express my opinions on what the animals might be. I had brought with me the skull that had generously been donated to me by Walt Andrus of MUFON, back in late 2008. It got almost as much coverage as I did. After the first round of filming, a call was made to Ryan Craighead, who was on the scene within the hour, along with a couple of friends. With the camera on him, Fox News recorded the details of his encounter and explained how he and some of his school buddies had seen the animal on a number of occasions, all prior to him having caught the creature on camera. He also explained that the gait of the creature reminded him most of all of that of a kangaroo. Having seen the photo, it was almost impossible to argue with that.

As night fell on Tecumseh, the Fox News team and I roamed the woods and fields in search of the creature. We actually did find fairly fresh coyote tracks and heard the distinct call of the coyote, too, but probably from a distance of a couple hundred yards, I would say. Five months after it first surfaced in Tecumseh, it seemed the town's resident chupacabra was determined to stay. We finished filming around 11:00 p.m. and, with the job completed, went our separate ways. The story wasn't quite over, however.

New Leads Develop

In many ways, it was not just what happened on that night in Tecumseh, Oklahoma, that was so intriguing, but what occurred afterwards. The story was soon broadcast on the local KOKH Fox 25 channel. Then, just a few weeks later, it was uploaded to the channel's website for one and all to see. Although the footage lasted for just a few minutes, a good job was done of condensing those four or five hours of filming into something that was both coherent and entertaining. The footage did something else, too. When it hit the Internet, it prompted three people to contact me. All of them were from Norman and all three had intriguing stories to relate.

Notably, two of the people had seen the strange creature that Ryan Craighead photographed (or, at least, they had encountered one that very much looked like it), one several months before his encounter and the other one just a few days prior to the filming. The second of the two callers described a hairless, coyote-like animal that ran like a regular coyote at times, but that occasionally broke into weird, brief, semi-upright hops, something that Craighead had noted too and caught on film. But it was the third story that really stood out in the high-strangeness stakes. It came from a woman I'll refer to as Shelley. Her account was one that, if true, suggested that at least some Texas chupacabra cases had far more to do with the domain of the paranormal than the regular world around us. After Shelley e-mailed me, outlining the story, I wasted no time in making a return trip to Tecumseh. Now, you'll see why.

Shape-Shifting on the Highway

Shelley and I agreed to meet up at the very same barbecue joint where I had rendezvoused with the Fox News crew; it was easy to find and the food was excellent. As we ate our late lunch, Shelley told me that she had lived in the area all of her life, and that her daughter attended Tecumseh High School. And, as a result, Shelley was often at the school. On one occasion, in June 2009, she was driving along the OK-9 E road, which links the towns of Norman and Tecumseh, when something truly extraordinary occurred. Out of the trees, on the right-hand side of the road, loomed what was undeniably a Texas chupacabra—a gray-blue, skinny, hairless beast that could have passed for the absolute twin of the Elmendorf Beast. Whereas Devin McAnally's encounter in Elmendorf was with an animal of purely flesh and blood proportions, this did not seem to be the case with the thing that Shelley had the profound misfortune to encounter.

Since it was around 10:00 a.m. when Shelley's sighting occurred, she said, the road was quiet; the school runs were over and most people were at work. Rather oddly, but also intriguingly, when Shelley slowed down, amazed by the sight of the creature that stood around sixty feet to her right, she felt a sudden, foreboding sense of isolation, of almost being in a vacuum, of being in a situation that … wasn't quite right.

For around a minute or more, said Shelley, the animal stared intently at her, which gave her the chills and a distinct feeling that it was trying to communicate with her. But what happened immediately afterwards upped the weird stakes to an incredible level. The animal sauntered across OK-9 E and, as it did so, something astounding occurred. It started to shimmer and blur. For a second or so, it appeared to take on the lumbering form of a small bear, then what appeared to be a sleek black cat, before finally returning to its original form of a chupacabra!

Bearing in mind that this all occurred at the height of summer, I asked Shelley if it was possible that what appeared to be a mutation of the animal's physical form might actually have been caused by a rippling, sizzling heat-haze on the road ahead of her. Shelley was absolutely sure that was not the case. She insisted that the creature she saw literally and briefly shape-shifted, although, I must make it clear, she did not use that emotive and inflammatory terminology. Stunned by what was going down, Shelley simply sat and stared as the animal wandered into the trees on the opposite side of the road and vanished, never to resurface.

That wasn't the only strange thing that happened. As she drove away, fairly shaken, Shelley turned on the radio. The song that was playing was Warren Zevon's song "Werewolves of London". No one, and that includes Shelley, needs to be told that werewolves are shape-shifters. The weirdness didn't end there. Later that day, Shelley had a call from an old school friend who was in the process of moving to Oregon and scouting around the area for potential homes. For no real reason, her friend happened to mention that a large black cat had been seen roaming around Deschutes County, the area to where she was moving. Shelley found all of this to be deeply strange. She had seen a coyote morph into a bear and a large cat, and then as the day progressed she found herself in situations involving just such a large cat on the other side of the country and shape-shifting monsters in London!

There was one other thing, too. It was something that Shelley was deeply embarrassed to admit, but she decided to go and tell me anyway (and, it's the main reason why Shelley asked me to change her name for the pages of this book). On the night of the encounter on OK-9 E, Shelley had an erotic dream about a coyote pursuing her across a harsh and hot desert environment before it had its savage way with her. I almost said, "Whatever floats your boat," but then I thought better of it. To Shelley, all of this seemed like some oddly surreal joke. I said to her that this might be exactly the case. With our lunch finished, we sat back in our chairs and I proceeded to tell Shelley a few strange tales about the coyote.

Things Get Tricky

Within Native American lore and legend, the coyote is defined by three things: its ability to take on the guise of other animals, its trickster-like character, and its sexual attraction to human women, the latter being something that may have had a bearing upon Shelley's dream. Within Navajo mythology, a male coyote will pursue a male hunter in the woods, then, when it closes in, it will magically throw its skin on the man. This allows the coyote to take control of the hunter and assume his appearance. The coyote does this to have sex with the man's wife or girlfriend, who fails to realize that the man she believes to be her husband is actually now something very different.

Synchronicities (or, meaningful coincidences, for those not familiar with the term) are staple parts of trickster encounters. That Shelley heard Warren Zevon's "Werewolves of London", only seconds after seeing one animal shape-shift into another is a perfect example of just such a synchronicity. As is the conversation that Shelley had with her old friend on the matter of a large black cat on the loose.

Within folklore, the coyote often plunges people into such strange situations as a means to teach them something, to elevate them, and to have them consider new paradigms and concepts. On the other hand, the coyote sometimes uses its trickster skills to bewilder, to puzzle and even to terrorize those it has in its beady, steely sights. Somewhat connected to all of this is the Yenaldlooshi, a hostile witch greatly feared by the Navajo, who wears the skin of a coyote. Deeply malevolent, the Yenaldlooshi is a cannibalistic devotee of necrophilia and is best avoided at all times, as if you couldn't figure that out on your own!

When I explained all of this to Shelley, she looked genuinely frightened. It was highly likely she had very good reason to be. She asked what she should do next. Given that Shelley had undergone a close encounter of the weird kind on the road, had experienced two profound synchronicities, and had a predatory, lust-filled coyote invade her dream, I offered that the best thing she could do would be to try and put everything behind her and move on with her life. She did exactly as I suggested; her experiences have not been repeated.

Part 3

CHUPACABRA CONSPIRACIES

Chapter 16

THE TEXAS CHUPACABRA AND AN UNDERGROUND BASE

2005 was a notable year for the chupacabra. In January of that year, the beast leapt from the real world into fiction, in a movie titled *Chupacabra: Dark Seas*, which was focused specifically on the Puerto Rican creature. When the movie was aired, I watched it eagerly. Well, at first I was eager. I was soon, however, bored— very bored. Lacking in suspense and tension, and filled with completely laughable special effects, it's a production I vowed never again to waste my time on—and, I'm very pleased to say, I haven't! *Chupacabra: Dark Seas* was not the worst movie about the beastly bloodsucker, however. That deeply dubious distinction goes to a 2013 disaster set in San Antonio, Texas, that I will return to later. Meanwhile, back to 2005 ...

What's a Wild Monkey Doing in Texas?
Good Question!

Situated a little less than two hundred miles from my Arlington, Texas, home is the city of Coleman. It's a distinctly small city too, with a population of fewer than six thousand. For such a tiny locale, Coleman is a place with a significant amount of high strangeness attached to it. As you can probably deduce, just from the fact that I'm referencing Coleman, the town plays a fairly large role in the chupacabra controversy. Before I get to all that, however, it's worth noting something else too. In fact, it's vital to note it, since it is part of the chupacabra story.

In 2000, a distinctly out-of-place monkey was shot and killed on a Coleman ranch by a Dallas hunter named Greg Martin. He said to the press at the time: "That was no organ-grinder monkey. That was a monkey that could grind your organs." Ouch!

It was big news in the area. The *Chronicle & Democrat Voice* newspaper ran nothing less than a front-page story on the killing of the monkey. It was a story accompanied by a photo of the monkey's head, which the hunter had sliced off for the camera. Welcome to Texas, y'all.

In some quarters the publication of the photo provoked outrage:

"I object to the lightheartedness shown at the death of the monkey," said Nancy Grimes, an irate reader of the newspaper, whose words were printed in its pages for all to see. "He (the monkey) had to be forced into such circumstances by the very species who ultimately killed him. Never again will I be able to enjoy the delightful antics of any monkey without those (newspaper) pictures coming to mind."

Greg Martin, whose bullet dropped the monkey from a distance of nearly four hundred feet, was unrepentant when approached by the press for comment: "After seeing the teeth on it and knowing it can be aggressive, I think I did the right thing, but mainly it was just out of place."

Jeff Bullock, the director of the Abilene Zoo, said to the newspaper that from the description, it sounded very much like either a Japanese snow monkey or a macaque. Precisely what it was doing in Coleman was just about anyone's guess, although, it's worth noting that sightings of the beast dated back not just years but decades, as Coleman's county clerk, JoAnn Hale, confirmed to the press. This is not at all impossible, since snow monkeys can live for around thirty years—that is, when they're not getting shot by hunters who proceed to chop off their heads.

"It's maddening that somebody would shoot it," said Hale, echoing the comments of Nancy Grimes.

It's actually not overly strange, or impossible, that a Japanese macaque just might turn up in the wilds of Texas. Around one hundred and fifty miles southwest of the Texas capital, Austin, is a very small town called Dilley. It is home to the Born Free USA Primate Sanctuary. And, in turn, the sanctuary is home to more than two hundred macaques, along with baboons and vervets; the latter is also known as African Green Monkeys. Some might consider it a stretch to suggest that a macaque could travel the two hundred sixty-plus miles from Dilley to Coleman, but it's not totally out of the question.

There is, however, something else to all of this, which is nothing less than a wild conspiracy theory that links the presence of the monkey directly to the matter of the chupacabra. It's important I point that fact out to you now, so you'll have an understanding of why the presence and the unfortunate death of the monkey are being mentioned in a book on allegedly blood-sucking vampires.

Five years after the controversial killing of the monkey occurred, a chupacabra was shot dead in Coleman. Mindful of the local public outrage that accompanied not just the shooting of the monkey, but also the way in which the story was reported, in 2005 the press trod very carefully and tactfully when it came to the matter of Coleman's dead chupacabra.

Mange or Not Mange?

October 2005 was when Coleman became blessed—if that's the right word to use—by a visit from something even stranger than an ultimately headless macaque. I know you know what it was.

"Bigfoot has not landed in Coleman County," said good-humored Stan Brudney, the co-publisher of the *Coleman Chronicle & Democrat-Voice*, when the story broke.

It was clear that something strange was going down. The newspaper stated that a local man, eighty-nine-year-old Reggie Lagow, had found a number of his chickens dead, some missing, others partially devoured, and all with nary a bit of blood in sight. This was not good news. The attacks continued and the chicken losses grew. Then whatever had targeted Lagow's animals focused its attentions on those of his neighbors too. But there was something else that was decidedly odd: both Lagow and his friends saw the animal, on more than a couple of occasions, quite clearly. The reason why they saw it is notable; the creature seemed to do all of its hunting and foraging in broad daylight, which is very odd and most atypical of the majority of wild animals in Texas, including, it must be stressed, coyotes.

The description of the beast was by now very familiar to everyone who had followed the chupacabra controversy: dog-like, skinny, and sporting an odd coating of hair. Not exactly mange, it was more akin to very soft and barely noticeable fuzz across its whole body. The back legs were longer than one would expect to see in a coyote, the front limbs were shorter than normal, the ears were huge, and the tail was almost surreally long. Attempts to identify the creature resulted in either puzzlement or a lack of solid agreement. Yes, it was clearly a canid, but even so, it was one that didn't just appear to be malnourished and mangy.

Despite having built a trap, Lagow had no luck in snaring the animal. Eventually, however, one of his neighbors had a distinct stroke of luck; the animal was shot dead as it invaded the man's chicken coop, ready to take yet even more terrified birds to the grave. When pictures were taken of the animal and highlighted by the media, even veterinarians were puzzled. One such veterinarian who lived near Lagow, Dr. Johnny Needham, admitted to the press that it looked odd, and acknowledged that the hair loss didn't seem to be what one would expect to see in a regular case of mange. He preferred to call it demodectic mange, which is a condition that is often caused when the animal has a severely compromised immune system. What might be causing such drastic effects upon the immune systems of the animals that have become known as Texas chupacabras is something we will return to in a later chapter.

The Conspiracy Theories Begin

In the fall of 2008, Ken Gerhard spent time in Coleman and had the good fortune to meet with then ninety-two-year-old Reggie Lagow. Ken also chatted with Dr. Needham, who was sure that whatever the Coleman creature was, a coyote it definitely was not. Lagow, a very sprightly nonagenarian who was mowing his lawn when Ken turned up at his home, told Ken that after the pictures of the animal's remains were taken, he had the body dumped, fearful of what animal-rights activists might do if they caught up with him. No doubt this fear was in part prompted by the furor and media coverage that surrounded the shooting and beheading of that mysterious monkey, roughly half a decade earlier.

There was something else, too. Lagow told Ken that, in his opinion, the animal was very likely the product of strange and futuristic government tinkering of the genetic kind. In a marvelously atmospheric fashion, one that would have easily befitted an old-time monster movie, filled with foggy moors, crashes of thunder, and bolts of lightning, Lagow (Ken's notes reveal) said the Coleman creature was "of two different kinds of flesh." Spawned and spliced by deranged scientists, its deadly kind were now on the loose in Texas.

A Texan Area 51—or Maybe Not

Not long after the story of the Coleman chupacabra surfaced in the media, I received a rather odd e-mail from a guy who claimed to know the truth behind the saga, which, he said, also explained the presence of the town's decapitated macaque. In other words, both animals—and both deaths—were somehow inextricably linked together. This better be good, I thought.

The man maintained that both animals had escaped from a futuristic lab that was buried deep below none other than the Coleman Municipal Airport! Well, that was quite an allegation to make. I asked for more data, only to receive a response suggesting it would not be wise to look into such matters, which immediately made me wonder why on earth the man had even bothered to share the information with me in the first place. Nevertheless, no matter how scant the data might have been, and how downright weird and unlikely the story was, I decided to look into it. This meant one thing, and one thing only: another road trip was in the cards.

When I arrived in Coleman, the first thing I did was to check out the airport. Its origins date back to 1941, when the military embarked on a program across Texas to create a series of installations where pilots could be trained. The Coleman Flying School was born, operated under the control of the United States Army Air Forces Gulf Coast Training Center. Such was the demand for pilots that followed the terrible December 1941 events at Pearl Harbor that at one point no fewer than two hundred aircraft and trainee pilots were on site. Above ground, it was a place of fairly significant size. But what about under the ground?

Entering a small, close-knit town in Texas can be a tricky thing; believe me, I know. When you start asking questions, the locals want to know why. They look at you in ways that can range from inviting to distrusting, and curious to hostile. Sometimes, the guns even come out. So, in an effort to be as open as I can be, I always tell it as it is. Just about everyone in the town, I learned, had heard about the chupacabra story, although none could really add anything that wasn't already being reported on by the local media and which is cited earlier in this chapter. Most people remembered the macaque affair too. No one knew a damned thing about secret labs below the airport. Undeterred, but not at all surprised, I decided to seize the bull by the horns and ask the airport staff about the story.

I was also not surprised that, as well as having no knowledge of such a top-secret facility, they found the whole thing very amusing. It was stressed to me that if the airport was sitting upon a highly classified installation of Area 51 proportions, one that was involved in secret research on monkeys and chupacabras, then surely there would be at least some evidence of such. They had a very good point; I could not argue with that. How did the employees of the secret base get to work without being seen? Where were the entrance points to the facility? Why had no one at the airport ever heard of such claims before? The questions were both valid and utterly reasonable. I didn't consider the journey to have been a wasted one, however, since I always feel that every lead should be followed up on, no matter how unlikely or wacky it might finally turn out to be. I headed home, leaving Coleman and its nonexistent, top-secret chupacabra research lab behind me. Or should that be probably nonexistent? That all depends upon one's own paranoia levels.

Personally, I seriously doubt there is anything below the Coleman Municipal Airport—aside from a hell of a lot of soil, spent bullets, and cow bones. The fear of chupacabra-based, nefarious activity of the conspiratorial and genetic kind in Texas, however, is something that Ken Gerhard was also exposed to during his Texas-based research, as he told me:

"One thing I hear about all the time is secret genetic testing going on. I think in the world we live in, it's easy for people to jump on that bandwagon that there's a covert agenda going on, and things are being manipulated in laboratories and here in Texas. But I don't see what the benefit of this testing would be. The most recent theory I've heard, which was kind of humorous and absurd at the same time, was that these Texas chupacabras were hunting dogs being used by aliens. It strikes me as odd that aliens would need hunting dogs in the first place, if they can travel through space and other dimensions. If they can do all that, why would they need hunting dogs?"

Why, indeed!

Chapter 17

MAKING A MONKEY
OUT OF VAMPIRES

They say that truth is stranger than fiction. And they are right, whoever "they" actually are. For me, at least, this really hit home on an expedition I made to Puerto Rico in 2010. To state that fantasy and reality collided in strange and surreal fashion would be an understatement. But let's start at the beginning and leave the surreal stuff for later. It was a Thursday afternoon in January, and, as so often happens, I got a telephone call out of the blue from a television production company that was interested in having me on a new documentary that was just about to be filmed. As I was soon to learn, however, the term "television production company" was far more than a bit of a stretch of the imagination.

It was the typical selling technique that I have come to know and hate over the years. It went something not unlike this: "We would love to have you fly out to Puerto Rico for a week. We don't have much of a budget, but we'll cover your flight and hotel room and throw in a meal or two. How's that sound, Nick?"

I replied that it sounded to me exactly like what it was: absolute, pure, and unadulterated bullshit. I explained that I don't work for free, and certainly not for a company that is planning to make a big-budget show for a major television channel. There was an audible gasp down the line, from what I soon learned was actually the producer's eighteen-year-old, unemployed girlfriend, who didn't know the difference between the chupacabra and Chappaquiddick. The gasp was followed by a brief silence and a promise to check in with the boss and see what could be done, or words to that effect, at least.

Yes, you go and do exactly that, I thought.

Very often, in such circumstances, I never hear a single word again. This time, however, was a very welcome change. The follow-up call was filled with apologies. A most suitable fee for my chupacabra-hunting skills was quickly negotiated, along with written confirmation that all of my expenses (that's to say flight, hotel room, food, and bar bills) would be paid in full, and confirmation that I would be allowed to wear my customary black T-shirts and black jeans and not be made to look like some wannabe Indiana Jones–style character, in camouflaged cargo pants, khaki shirt, and ridiculously floppy hat.

Then there came a somewhat unusual revelation; there was no production company or television channel in sight. There was just the girl at the end of the phone and her boyfriend— yes, the aforementioned boss. He, whom I will call Mark, was a twenty-one-year-old film student who had seen me on a 2009 Discovery Channel documentary on the chupacabra. It was a show in which I discussed the possibility that at least some chupacabra sightings may actually have been of rhesus monkeys, which certainly do live in Puerto Rico.

Mark was particularly taken by the rhesus monkey theory. As a result, his idea was to follow me around Puerto Rico for a week, with nothing but a handheld camera to record what went down. In other words, this was going to be akin to *The Blair Witch Project* for monster fans. While I thought it was a cool and alternative idea, alarms bells were already starting to go off in my head: One kid and a camera. No production company. An out-of-work girlfriend. This did not bode at all well for my fee. So I came straight to the point and told the pair that I would be pleased to get involved, but I wanted my money up front. As in every single cent and dollar of it. After a couple of days of waiting, during which, I later learned, Mark took out a loan from his parents, the money was transferred to my bank account. We were finally good to go.

So, flight tickets were quickly arranged and I packed a bag. Two days later, I flew from Dallas-Fort Worth International Airport to Florida, and then on to the island I had come to know and love so well. I arrived shortly after the sun had set in Puerto Rico's capital, San Juan, as the ocean waters twinkled under a bright moon. After sitting for hours on a stiflingly hot plane, and with nothing but warm beer and margaritas and sticky plastic glasses to pass the time of day, it was a magical sight to behold. Mark, who had flown in the day before, met me at the bustling airport. He was a beaming, long-haired, lanky kid who shared my love of punk rock, horror movies, and beer. We were going to get along just fine.

We ate a late dinner and had many laughs that night at the Wind Chimes Inn, which I'd suggested, given that I had stayed there on my first trip to Puerto Rico in the summer of 2004, with the SyFy Channel, and I knew that the food was excellent.

Mark's beam began to fade, however, when later, over drinks at the bar, I told him the story of how I got peed on by a potentially rabid bat in a Puerto Rican cave five years earlier, and of dicey confrontations with local and potentially lethal gangs of thugs. Then, when I told him of an encounter with the cops while investigating big cat reports in San Juan (about which, more in a later chapter), Mark went silent and into a thoughtful mode. From the look on his face, however, I'd say that panic mode was a far more accurate description.

"Welcome to Puerto Rico, mate!" I said, as Mark tried his very best to manage a weak smile but utterly failed.

But what of those rhesus monkeys and the potential chupacabra connection that so fascinated Mark?

Monkeying Around on the Island of Vampires

When Jon Downes and I rampaged around Puerto Rico for a week or so in 2004, time and again we heard a number of stories that essentially said that if we wanted to get the "real truth" about the chupacabra, we should turn our attentions away from matters relative to blood-sucking vampires, aliens, UFOs, and the world of the supernatural. Instead, it was suggested by more than a few people, we should go knocking on the door of something called the Caribbean Primate Research Center. The CPRC is located not in Puerto Rico itself, but on the tiny, very close-by island of Cayo Santiago, which is also known as Isla de los Monos, or Monkey Island. And when I say the island is tiny, we are talking about only approximately two thousand feet by one thousand, three hundred feet. And that's it. But for such a small place, it's one that is steeped to the max in intrigue and history.

The origins of the CPRC date back to the 1930s. That was when a group of rhesus monkeys was shipped to Cayo Santiago from India, and when and where a wide variety of medical experimentation began in earnest. Today, there are almost one thousand rhesus monkeys on the island, nearly all of which live in the open and which are relatively tame. The staff of the CPRC notes on its official website that this particular line of work is focused on "the study and use of non-human primates as models for studies of social and biological interactions and for the discovery of methods of prevention, diagnosis and treatment of diseases that afflict humans."

One of the most notable and important areas of research undertaken at the CPRC is that concerning SIV. It is the simian equivalent of HIV, which in humans can lead to full-blown Acquired Immunodeficiency Syndrome, or AIDS. It's in the heart of the CPRC's Virology Laboratory on Cayo Santiago that the work is undertaken. And it's all very worthwhile and has led to important breakthroughs in combating the disease.

There is, however, something else, too. There are rumors of other, far more secret labs in Puerto Rico itself, about labs buried deep within (and, some say, maybe even deep below) Puerto Rico's huge El Yunque rain forest, and which have nothing to do with the far more down-to-earth work undertaken on Cayo Santiago. It's there, supposedly, where hideous experimentation of a gene-manipulating kind has been clandestinely undertaken on rhesus monkeys and that has led to the creation of ghoulish, violent monsters. And do I really need to tell you what those same manmade monsters are assumed by many to be? That's right: chupacabras.

In essence, that was the story told to Jon Downes and me in 2004. The vampiric chupacabra was actually born out of crazed gene tinkering and mutated monkeys. Back then, due to the rigid time schedules of the SyFy Channel, Jon and I weren't able to do anything in the way of research, at all, into this particular area. Half a decade later, however, things were very different. Mark had researched similar stories and was interested in pursuing this particular theory above all others, which was fine with me.

The Vampire of Moca

Luckily, I still had the contact information for four of the people who had made observations to Jon and me on this very subject in 2004. While two of the contacts unfortunately proved impossible to trace (their phone numbers were no longer active and checks with the SyFy Channel turned out to be utterly futile), the remaining two were eager to chat. One of them was a woman named Guanina. She lived in Moca, situated on the west side of the island, founded in 1772 by one Don Jose de Quinonez.

It had been six years since I had first briefly met Guanina, but I told Mark I would give her a call and see if we could get things moving. Fortunately, she remembered me; we had a laugh on the phone about how, back in 2004, all the kids in the neighborhood had come running out to see what was going on when we did a bit of background filming on the outskirts of Moca. Guanina had been a godsend; she and her husband ran a small café and had generously supplied us with plenty of water and soda as the cameras rolled under a merciless sun.

Around 2:00 p.m. on the afternoon of our first day of investigation, Mark and I arrived at the café. Guanina gave me a big hug, thrust a cold can of Sprite into my hand, and dished up platefuls of mofongo for Mark and me. Guanina, forty-some-thing, dark-haired, and tanned, had an interesting theory about a creature that, back in the mid-1970s, became briefly legendary in the area. It was known as the Moca Vampire. It was a theory, however, that dated back to around 1987. Mark, barely able to contain himself, eagerly set up his camera and started rolling, as Guanina and I settled back in our chairs to chat.

Murderous Monkeys on the Loose

A teenager back in 1987, Guanina used to enjoy walking the hills around Moca. That is, however, until a decidedly traumat-ic, and even horrific, experience occurred in May 1987 and put paid to all of that. As she strolled around the pathways, Guani-na suddenly heard the unmistakable screech of a pig in distress. She raced up the hill, forty or fifty feet or so, and was confront-ed by a shocking sight: Six or seven monkeys were viciously attacking the poor pig, which by now was on the ground and clearly close to being in mortal danger.

Guanina shouted at the monkeys, which suddenly ceased their attack and turned their eyes away from the pig and onto Guanina. For a second or two, there was a tense standoff. For-tunately, however, the monkeys merely made violent, scream-ing chatter and then raced away into the deeper grass of the hill. Equally fortunately, the pig, although obviously traumatized, un-steadily rose to its feet, stood around for a few minutes, presum-ably trying to get its bearings, and then wandered off into the un-dergrowth. Not surprisingly, a terrified Guanina raced down the hill to the safety of her home.

When Guanina told her parents what she had just seen, all three decided to look into the matter further. Scanning various books in the local library, they were soon able to identify the attacking animals as rhesus monkeys. There were, however, two things that quite rightly puzzled the family. Although there are hundreds of rhesus monkeys on the nearby island of Cayo Santiago at the Caribbean Primate Research Center, there should not have been any on mainland Puerto Rico. Plus, rhesus monkeys live chiefly on fruit, cereal, and seeds. Occasionally, they will eat bugs and grubs. They are not, however, noted for launching concerted, savage attacks on fully grown pigs. Or, more correctly, normal rhesus monkeys aren't known for doing that. And here's where we get to the crux of the sinister saga.

A Tale Worthy of *The X-Files*

Guanina told her story to a number of people over the years, including a veterinarian in Moca, who quietly shared some notable information with her. It was all highly conspiratorial, but according to Guanina's source, the military had been doing some distinctly controversial research at a fortified underground lab somewhere in the El Yunque rain forest. The purpose of the research was to try and determine if animals could be utilized on battlefields as nothing less than weapons of war. And how exactly, might such a thing be achieved? Simply by infecting the animals with an engineered viral cocktail that would alter their mindsets and turn them into homicidal killers. As for which animals might prove to be the most profitable, they were monkeys and apes. The veterinarian speculated that, just perhaps, some of those same monkeys escaped from the lab, made their way to Moca, and took out their rage on a pig that was unlucky enough to get in their way.

Well, this was a great story, one that Mark loved and which I found to be highly intriguing. But the story was something else, too; it was deeply familiar. The idea of creating violent behavior in monkeys and apes by injecting them with a virus designed to turn their fairly placid characters into those of homicidal killers was presented to the world in 2002 in a mega-hit movie. Its title was *28 Days Later*.

In the movie (the success of which provoked an equally successful sequel, *28 Weeks Later*), monkeys and apes infected with what is termed the "Rage Virus" are released from a secret lab in England by animal-rights activists. In no time at all the virus jumps to the human population. As a result, the United Kingdom quickly becomes a land filled with crazed, zombie-like maniacs with just one aim on what is left of their minds, which is to infect and slaughter anyone who crosses their paths. Guanina earnestly assured me that she heard the story no later than 1988. Was it a clear case of fact eerily mirroring fiction, or vice versa? That's what Guanina suggested, when I told her of *28 Days Later*, a movie she claimed not to have seen.

For Guanina, this was the answer to both the Moca Vampire and the chupacabra: they were rhesus monkeys, ones that were probably secretly brought over from the island of Cayo Santiago, infected with who knows what, savagely transformed into violent, raging killers, and then let loose to gauge how profitable they might be if unleashed on the battlefield against enemy troops.

In all likelihood, suggested Guanina, if the program was deemed worthy, it would be far bigger and more powerful animals that would be used in warfare—most probably fully grown chimpanzees. They certainly can inflict major damage upon a person, even without the benefit of the Rage Virus coursing through their veins. The rhesus monkeys, she opined, were probably used solely at the experimental stage, for two, admittedly logical, reasons: They were very easy to secure from nearby Cayo Santiago; being of fairly short stature, they were pretty easy to handle. True or not, it was a great way to start the filming. We said our goodbyes and hit the road back to San Juan for an evening of dinner and discussion.

The following day was spent interviewing me, chiefly to secure my thoughts on Guanina's account and theories, and then to plan the next excursion, a trip to the Puerto Rican city of Ponce, where we were to meet with Benigno Munoz, a farmer with a similar tale to tell.

Slaughter in Ponce

Ponce is the second biggest city in Puerto Rico. A bustling metropolis, Ponce has origins that date back to the sixteenth century when the Taino tribe held sway over the area, although not for long. After the Spanish warrior-explorer Juan Ponce de Leon reached Puerto Rico in 1508, the countdown to conquest was well and truly on. Sadly, the all-too-trusting Taino people fell victim to the manipulative, power-hungry Spaniards and in no time at all the old days were gone. Both a new age and a new city were destined to rise up. And they did.

While Ponce is not known for its repeated sightings of the chupacabra, in 1992 a spate of animal killings occurred in the suburbs of the city that suggested the Moca Vampire had moved on to pastures new. In other words, animals—cats, dogs, chickens, and pigs—were found drained of the red stuff, *The Strain*–style, no less. Since the killings predated, by a couple of years, the 1995 surfacing of the chupacabra, the matter did not get the publicity that it would otherwise have very likely achieved a few years later.

It was purely down to chance that I got to meet Benigno back in 2004. He was the brother-in-law of one of the local crew that the SyFy Channel had hired to work on the episode of *Proof Positive* that Jon Downes and I were there to be filmed for. When Benigno's brother-in-law mentioned over breakfast one day that we should really speak to him, and he outlined exactly why, I knew we were onto a winner. Well, no, actually, we weren't. Time was of the essence, but I assured Benigno in a quick phone call that one day I would be back to Puerto Rico and then it would be time to address his story in full. Finally, now was that time.

Mark and I had to wait until Friday night before we had the opportunity to speak with Benigno; his work as a farmer came first, which was only right. After all, he had a living to earn, and chatting about blood-sucking monsters was not exactly going to bring in the dollars for him. Just like Guanina, Benigno was incredibly hospitable. He and his wife, Julia, prepared for us a feast fit for kings, one that was filled with all kinds of local culinary delights, not to forget the amazing homemade mango margaritas.

The Conspiracy Theories Continue to Flow

It was most interesting that Benigno and Guanina were totally unknown to each other, since their stories were extremely similar in nature. Mark, grinning from ear to ear, set up his camera and started filming. Whereas Guanina wasn't sure of the exact location where all the diabolical experimentation supposedly took place, Benigno was absolutely certain he did know.

It was a now closed-down United States Navy base, Roosevelt Roads. It opened up shop in the 1940s and became a hub for target practice operations. Base personnel, however, had an uneasy and strained relationship with the people of Puerto Rico for years, to the extent that the base finally closed its doors in early 2004.

According to Benigno, he had a friend in the U.S. Navy who told him of bizarre and top secret experimentation, reportedly undertaken in a bunker-like environment below Roosevelt Roads, which was focused on controlling the minds of monkeys and apes, yet again to determine exactly how homicidal the animals could be made. Apparently, the disturbing answer was: extremely homicidal. Benigno had heard other stories too; they suggested all manner of apes and monkeys were being secretly flown in from various parts of the world, and all of which became the victims of terrible and unethical testing.

Most of the initial experiments, Benigno's Navy friend had told him, were carried out on small monkeys, those that could easily be handled and contained. Reportedly, when full-grown chimpanzees were mutated into something horrific, armed guards were on hand at all times. And that was it. A fascinating story, and certainly a highly controversial one, about how and why secret experiments of a genetic and viral variety had spawned what was now an unstoppable vampire legend.

There was something else, too. Something amazing.

Captured, Caged, and Caught on Camera

When he finished relating his account, Benigno motioned Mark and me to follow him outside. He pointed to a large cage that sat just outside the end of his backyard. I wish I could say that it contained a violent killer chimpanzee with a lust for copious amounts of human blood, but it did not. What it did contain, however, was a cotton-top tamarin, a small monkey that is native to Colombia, South America. It takes its name from the mane of white hair that dominates its head. I asked Benigno where he got it from, to which he replied, in the field behind his house, about five months previously.

Now, admittedly, this was not as exciting as finding a rage-infected, murderous monkey or a crazed, anger-filled ape, but the fact is that there should not be any cotton-top tamarins living wild anywhere in Puerto Rico. Incredibly, however, that seemed to be exactly what was going on. Needless to say, no one could mistake this little creature for a marauding, vampire-like beast, but its presence did bolster the theories of both Guanina and Benigno that monkeys were brought to the island, had escaped from their military masters, and soon made new lives for themselves in the wild. If the smaller, uninfected monkeys, similar to those which lived quite happily on land just adjacent to Benigno's yard, were on the loose, then just maybe their highly infected comrades of a much larger kind were also roaming around. And maybe they had helped to spawn the stories of the chupacabra.

What was a cotton-top tamarin monkey doing in Puerto Rico?
Good question!

On the next morning, our last day on the island, Mark and I returned to Benigno and Julia's home and he offered to show us exactly where he found the monkey, which was clearly very used to being around people, since it raced over and jumped onto his shoulder when he opened the cage and motioned it to come to him.

Knowing that Mark wanted to get some good footage, Benigno suggested to Mark that he should film me wandering around the field with his loaded pistol in hand. Mark looked a bit ashen. He was clearly not someone used to handling weapons. Fortunately, as a resident of pistol-packing Texas, I am. Should anyone ever decide to break into my apartment, they will live to regret it. Or, they'll just regret it. But I digress. Back to the story. So, taking Benigno up on his suggestion, we secured a great deal of footage of me clambering around and waving the pistol just about here, there, and everywhere. We didn't see any monkeys, rage-free or infected, but at least Mark was getting the footage he needed.

That night, back at the hotel, hours were spent discussing what we had achieved over the course of the past week. Mark was very pleased with the footage, the interviewees, and my sound-bites on the theory that, just maybe, some chupacabra reports were due to the deranged actions of virally affected apes and monkeys, rather than literal monsters. I stressed to Mark that while I thought such a theory might explain some of the sightings and attacks of the blood-draining kind, there were other reports that were far less easy to reconcile. And that was it. Seven days of good food, fine booze, tales that were part amazing and part disturbing, and a new and unique look at the creature of the island.

As for what happened next, well, that's a whole different story. Mark kept in touch with me over the course of the weeks that followed and was enthusiastic about trying to sell his production to one of the major channels, such as Animal Planet, Discovery, or History. A few months later, however, Mark and his girlfriend suddenly split; I never did learn why. Deep depression set in on

Mark's part, and thereafter I heard from him less and less. The last occasion was in January 2012, when, out of the blue, he called to say he had placed the project and the footage on hold.

And on hold is apparently where it continues to languish to this very day. I still, however, have hopes that maybe one day the results of that week in Puerto Rico when Mark and I made monkeys out of the chupacabra will finally surface.

Chapter 18

CRASHED UFOS, A SECRET
BASE, AND A CERTAIN MONSTER

There can be very few, if indeed any, people with an interest in paranormal phenomena that have not heard of the infamous Roswell UFO crash of July 1947. According to the story, it was on the massive Foster Ranch (situated in Lincoln County, New Mexico, and a couple of hours' drive from Roswell) that in early July the U.S. military secretly scooped up the remains of a wrecked craft from another world and its dead crew of large-headed, dwarfish pilots. While staff at the Roswell Army Air Field busied themselves by assuring the press that it was all a big mistake, and that nothing stranger than a weather balloon had fallen to earth, the legend goes that the mangled bodies and the debris were secretly flown to a military base in Dayton, Ohio. Its name was Wright Field. Today, it's known as Wright-Patterson Air Force Base.

Wright-Pat's reputation as the number-one resting place for alien entities with distinctly bad flying skills is legendary. Insiders and whistleblowers talk about Hangar 18, Building 18, and the Blue Room. All three are supposedly distinctly off-limits rooms, buildings, and underground bunkers where the carefully preserved remains of who knows how many dead extraterrestrials can be found, if one has the correct, high-level security.

It turns out that Puerto Rico has its very own equivalent, the Roosevelt Roads Naval Station. For many years, it acted as the island's very own Blue Room—reportedly, it's important to stress. But it wasn't alien bodies that were cryogenically housed at Roosevelt Roads. Nope. It was a bunch of dead chupacabras. There just might even have been a couple of living ones there too. So I was told. I was not surprised to find that sifting fact from fiction, and legend from rumor, proved to be no easy job when it came to trying to unravel the controversial truth about Roosevelt Roads' chupacabra stash. It was, however, a job that had to be done. But before I get to the matter of those allegedly dead vampires on ice, a quick and concise lesson in history is required.

A Military Presence Is Born

The origins of Roosevelt Roads date back to just one year after the end of the First World War. It was 1919 when the then Assistant Secretary of the U.S. Navy visited Puerto Rico. That man was none other than future American president Franklin D. Roosevelt. The visit was no vacation, however. Roosevelt was there on a secret mission. He was focused on finding a suitable location where a military facility could be constructed, one that could act as a strategic outpost for Uncle Sam in the Caribbean. Roosevelt toured the island, finally pinpointing a northeast town called Ceiba, which was founded back in the 1830s, and that today has a population of around thirteen thousand.

At the time, while the creation of such a base with an airfield could have been beneficial, it was not perceived as absolutely crucial. Things changed dramatically, however, when Adolf Hitler came to power in 1930s-era Germany. The world was soon to face complete and utter chaos, the likes of which it had never before seen. Steps had to be taken to combat the Nazi threat. One of those steps was the creation of Roosevelt Roads, which began in 1940, one year before the terrible events at Pearl Harbor, Hawaii, occurred.

Roosevelt Roads ultimately became the biggest U.S. Navy base on the planet and the headquarters of the U.S. Naval Forces Southern Command (NAVSO). It remained so for decades. All that changed, however, in March 2004, when NAVSO was given a new home, the Jacksonville, Florida-based naval station Mayport. The closure of the base was perceived by the people of Puerto Rico as a double-edged sword. On the one hand, the presence of the base provided a great deal of revenue for the people of Puerto Rico in general and of Ceiba in particular. On the other hand, those striving for complete independence on the island saw the base's closure as a good thing.

Now, with that said, it's time to take a look at the story of Roosevelt Roads' role as a top-secret storage area for chupacabras. Or, maybe, an alleged top-secret storage area.

Puerto Rico's Very Own Roswell—or Two

As you'll come to learn later, on our visit to Puerto Rico in July 2004, Jon Downes and I heard a story of a UFO crash in the hills of Canovanas in 1957, one which reportedly, and quickly, led to gross mutations in the local populace. It was not a stand-alone story, however. On his first trek around the island, in 1998, Jon himself was given no less than five independent accounts of this 1957 event. One of Jon's sources was a man named Reuben, a Puerto Rican brought up in New York, but who returned to the island as an adult. Arguably, Reuben was Jon's most significant source, since he personally took Jon and the Channel 4 TV crew to the very spot in Canovanas where, he claimed, the craft from another world slammed into the ground, back in 1957.

Jon told me that they came to a big clearing where the path became narrow and on one side disappeared altogether into a huge saucer-shaped arena. This, according to what Reuben had to say at least, was where the UFO had crashed. Admittedly, there was a huge indent in the side of the mountain, said Jon. No trees grew there, and it did look as if some huge object had crashed into the mountain, scooping out trees and vegetation and leaving a bare area intermittently covered with patchy grass.

Moving ahead six years, to 2004, it turned out that none other than Anna, of the 1975 chupacabra encounter in El Yunque, had heard of this 1957 tale too. This was not surprising, given that it's hardly an unknown case among the people of Puerto Rico. Anna told Jon and me that most people identified the location as a steep hillside in Canovanas, one that U.S. military forces quickly sealed off, for a period of around three weeks. Time constraints unfortunately prevented us from taking Anna to the location identified by Reuben back in 1998, but Anna's description of the place strongly suggested they were one and the same. There was something else too. Most of those that had commented on the incident, albeit briefly, said that when the UFO was accessed by the military they found within it the dead bodies of a number of unearthly creatures: chupacabras.

Jon and I had to remember that although the crash report had been around for decades, the chupacabra aspect of the story surfaced specifically post-1995, when the goat-sucking phenomenon began in earnest. The chupacabra link to the 1957 crash was fascinating, but it would have been even more fascinating had it surfaced prior to the 1995 outbreak. That it specifically didn't kept Jon and me mindful of the possibility that this was an elaboration, a new twist, on an old tale, though not necessarily a deliberate and deceitful one.

There is also a story of a UFO crashing in the heart of El Yunque in February 1984. I know that because the basics of the account have reached me on three occasions over the past decade. It was early one morning when a large, circular-shaped object slammed into the ground, immediately after flying over the rain forest in a decidedly erratic fashion. To prevent people from learning the truth of the matter, a diversionary tactic was put into place that the UFO was a meteorite. Personnel from NASA, the U.S. Air Force, and the CIA were soon on the scene, in part to scoop up the pummeled body parts of a couple of dead chupacabras, whose lives came to sudden and bloody ends when the alien craft hurtled violently into the forest at high speed. That's how the story goes, anyway.

I mention these two cases because there are claims that the bodies recovered from both the 1957 and 1984 incidents were secretly transported to Roosevelt Roads for study and autopsy by senior U.S. Navy medical personnel, in a deeply buried, fortified bunker, no less. Reportedly, at least some of the bodies were later taken to an unidentified military base in Florida.

A Very Close Encounter

There is another reason why I was so intrigued by the potential UFO link to the chupacabra controversy. It was because of something that happened back in 2004. Shortly after the *Proof*

Positive shoot was completed for the SyFy Channel, I spoke with a woman who had her own encounter with a UFO, but in a location where a chupacabra was seen only days later.

As Rosario told me, it was early March 2000, and she was working in a grove near the foot of El Yunque where she picked plantains. Her attention was suddenly drawn to a deep, resonating hum coming from directly above her.

Looking up, Rosario was startled to see a black, triangular-shaped object, about twenty-five to thirty-five feet in length, that was hovering overhead at a height estimated to be around ninety to one hundred and twenty feet, and which had a glossy, shiny surface. Surprise and amazement turned to shock when a pencil-thin beam of light shot out of the base of the craft, fanned out, and enveloped Rosario in a pink glow.

For what seemed like an eternity, Rosario was rooted to the spot, while her mind was flooded with images of widespread nuclear destruction and environmental collapse in the Earth's near future. The final image was of a large, bald head with huge, black eyes that closely resembled the alien face on the cover of Whitley Strieber's 1987 best-selling book *Communion*, which Rosario was inexplicably drawn to read in the immediate aftermath.

Suddenly, the light retracted and the flying triangle rose into the sky, heading slowly towards the heart of the rain forest. Interestingly, in the wake of the encounter, Rosario developed an overwhelming interest in environmental issues, and quite literally overnight, after a lifetime of eating meat, became a staunch advocate of vegetarianism.

That was not all. Three days later, and only a couple of hundred feet from where Rosario was working on that fateful day, two girls spotted a chupacabra of the bipedal, spiked, and decidedly menacing kind. The beast spotted them too. Evidently, however, it was a monster on a mission; after peering at them for a few moments it fell down on all fours and bounded away into the heavy undergrowth. It was an event that, due to both the time frame and the proximity, led Rosario to conclude the chupacabra was somehow linked to the UFO phenomenon. And here's the clincher: she too had heard rumors of dead chupacabra found in a crashed UFO some years earlier that had been secretly taken to Roosevelt Roads.

Also of relevance, while in Puerto Rico in 2005 with Paul Kimball and his Red Star Films crew, our guide, Orlando, was filmed talking about a 1990s-era event in which U.S. military forces reportedly captured several extremely vicious chupacabra in El Yunque. What happened to them, beyond first being held at Roosevelt Roads and then flown on to the United States in secure cages aboard a military aircraft, is unknown. And then there was that 2010 story of alleged classified experiments undertaken on monkeys and apes in an underground facility at the base that I described earlier.

Was this all nothing stranger than modern day folklore in the making? Or could it have been the cold, stark truth? Was Roosevelt Roads really a Puerto Rican equivalent of Wright-Patterson Air Force Base's Blue Room? In May 2011, I decided to do a bit of digging. If there were answers, they needed to be found.

Chapter 19

THE ROOSEVELT ROADS AFFAIR

I have always found that no matter where I'm traveling and whatever anomaly I'm pursuing, the best way to find information is to simply walk up to people and ask for it. Stores, bars, newspaper offices, restaurants, gas stations—they often prove to be the perfect places to uncover a few things of significance—and sometimes a lot of things. And, in terms of the latter, that was exactly the case in Ceiba, the town that for so many years was home to the Roosevelt Roads Naval Station.

I learned pretty quickly that many of the people of Ceiba had a lot of good things to say about Roosevelt Roads, such as the fact that the presence of the base had certainly helped the community to prosper, both financially and socially. Others were clearly far less enthused and felt that the presence of the base amounted to nothing less than a full-blown military occupation; they were overjoyed when, in 2004, Roosevelt Roads closed its doors forever. More than a few people had no firm opinion one way or the other. They just went about their lives, not giving it much thought at all.

A couple of people told me tales of 1990s-era chupacabra sightings in the Ceiba Forest, which is a small, wooded area dominated by mangrove trees, situated about five miles outside of Ceiba itself. The reports were scant in data and revolved around nighttime attacks on chickens and goats, and, of course, of the ubiquitous sucking of vast amounts of blood. There was also a tale of a pig found dead and disemboweled early one morning on a Ceiba street in 1999 or thereabouts.

Interestingly, all of the people who had something negative to say, usually loudly, about the alleged dark activity going on within Roosevelt Roads were those who openly held grudges against the U.S. military presence on the island. On the other hand, not a single, solitary person who spoke positively about the old naval base had anything even remotely relevant to the chupacabra phenomenon to relate. In that sense, the deeper the grudge, the much stronger the belief was that the U.S. Navy just had to have been up to no good and up to its neck in monster conspiracies.

A perceptive psychologist could probably deduce a great deal from all of that.

Vampires in the Tunnels

Certainly the most interesting piece of data I uncovered on what was a very brief trip to the island surfaced in a local bar after sunset and when the alcohol was flowing down the throats of the locals at a particularly furious pace. There was a rumor of vast, cavernous, underground tunnels deep below Roosevelt Roads. When the U.S. Navy said its goodbyes in 2004, it neglected to tell the people of Ceiba that something terrifying was on the loose in those dark tunnels, something that had escaped from its confines—a violent pack of chupacabras. The Navy, I was informed, took the approach that as they were heading off for pastures new, the creatures were now Ceiba's problem and not theirs, should they ever surface.

I couldn't fail to find it significant that my source for this story (a middle-aged man named Feredo) revealed that back in the late 1980s he had taken part in a number of Ceiba-based anti-American demonstrations. They were all based around concerns that Roosevelt Roads was recklessly pumping hazardous waste into the local water supply.

As engaging as Feredo's story of a vicious pack of underground chupacabras was, it was obvious that he was using it as a means to try and convince me of what he perceived as the evil nature of the government and military of the United States of America. I wasn't buying into his political agenda at all. Nor was I impressed by his attempts to turn a discussion of the chupacabra into what was a full blown anti-American rant. Just maybe, however, I bought into his tale of tunnel-dwelling, blood-drinking nightmares, at least to a small degree. I have to grudgingly admit that when it comes to the world of the unknown, even I'm not totally free of Fox Mulder's "I want to believe" approach.

As a brief aside, while I was still in Ceiba I heard a second-hand tale of a chupacabra allegedly seen in the early 2000s. It was doing nothing less than scaling a huge observation tower that stands proud and tall in the El Yunque rain forest and which provides a panoramic view of miles of amazing scenery. I know, since I have climbed its steps many times. It's called the Yokahu Tower and was constructed in 1963. The story was that a couple of American tourists had just exited the tower late one afternoon when they heard a strange squawking noise coming from the far side of the tower. They tentatively took a look, only to be confronted by a large, hairless, monkey-like animal that sported small, near-vestigial wings, a bald head, blood-red eyes, and long and bony limbs. It made an amazing leap onto the side of the tower and gripped its surface with its powerful claws. At a height of about twenty-five feet, it leapt into the surrounding trees and was lost from sight.

The Yokahu Tower, the haunt of the goat sucker.

It was, for me, yet another of those take it or leave it moments.

On the Move

Two months after my latest trip to Puerto Rico, the chupacabra reared its ugly head again, this time, however, in none other than Russia. In July 2011, the *Moscow News* reported:

"A blood-sucking creature is preying upon goats near Novosibirsk. As rational explanations run thin on the ground, the specter of the so-called chupacabra raises its demon head. Horrified farmers and smallholders are confronted by the drained corpses of their livestock in the morning, bloodless and bearing puncture marks to the neck but otherwise largely intact. But local cops are reluctant to record apparent vampire attacks, as they await official recertification, leaving the locals up in arms."

Conventional theories for the attacks ranged from packs of wild dogs to occultists. It was, however, the theory that the chupacabra had made its way to Russia that was the firm favorite with the locals. And things didn't end there. The commie vampire was far from done with terrorizing the land of the far less than free—as you'll soon see.

Chapter 20

THE CHUPACABRA
FROM A LAND DOWN UNDER?

Now and again, I find myself on the receiving end of a conspiratorial story that is so unbelievable, so downright bizarre, and so utterly implausible that I actually wish it could be true, even though it isn't. Well...it probably isn't. Or is it? I still can't be sure. In terms of the chupacabra, I was in just such a position in September 2013. That was when, on the third of the month, I received the first of around twenty e-mails from a man I'll call Ed. It transpires that Ed, who lived in Utah and who claimed to work at the ultra-secret Dugway Proving Ground, had seen the 2004 episode of the SyFy Channel's *Proof Positive* series—not when it was first aired, but when it was uploaded to YouTube in 2012 and where it can still be viewed to this day. Ed said he could tell me exactly what the chupacabras were, and so I said words to the effect of "Please tell me." He certainly did that and much more besides.

According to Ed, the creatures that have become known as chupacabras amount to nothing less than relic populations of thylacines. And what, you may well ask, are thylacines? Well, I'll tell you. Their correct name is *Thylacinus cynocephalis*, which translates as pouched dog with a wolf's head. They are dog-sized, striped marsupials, with jaws that have the ability to open to almost one hundred and eighty degrees. There is, however, a problem with this theory. Actually, there are two (at least!). Thylacines are believed to have become extinct back in the 1930s, and they were native to New Guinea, Australia, and Tasmania, none of which is anywhere remotely near the island of Puerto Rico. That was okay, though; that fact didn't have a single bearing upon Ed's engagingly odd scenario.

"They Walked on Their Toes like a Dog but Could Also Move in a More Unusual Way—a Bipedal Hop"

Before I get to Ed's story, a bit of background on the thylacine is very much in order. Although, as I noted above, mainstream zoology is of the opinion the creature is now extinct, it most certainly had a good run. Fossilized examples of the creature have been found, demonstrating that it lived as far back as the Miocene period. That's to say, around twenty-three million to five million years ago. While the thylacine is generally accepted to have died out in Australia thousands of years ago, history has shown it clung on in Tasmania, roughly one hundred and fifty miles from Australia, until quite recently. Not everyone, however, is so sure the creature is completely gone. How do we know? All thanks to the Tasmania Parks and Wildlife Service (TPWS) and the Australian government's Freedom of Information Act, that's how.

Both the TPWS and the Australian government have declassified their files and records on the creature. They are filled with credible sightings of thylacines in Tasmania, all of which post-date the 1930s, and in some cases significantly so. In the TPWS's own words:

> Since 1936, no conclusive evidence of a thylacine has been found. However, the incidence of reported thylacine sightings has continued. Most sightings occur at night, in the north of the State, in or near areas where suitable habitat is still available. Although the species is now considered to be "probably extinct," these sightings provide some hope that the thylacine may still exist.

The Australian government notes:

> Australia is home to some of the world's most unusual and mysterious wildlife. Our native animals, such as the platypus, the koala and the kangaroo, have been a source of wonder and surprise to people the world over. But perhaps our most mysterious animal is the thylacine, or Tasmanian Tiger. There are many reasons why people are fascinated by this animal. Perhaps it is its name and the romantic notion of Australia having its own "tiger." Perhaps it is its sad history since European settlement, or the fact that there are many people who claim they have seen a Tasmanian Tiger and believe it may not be extinct after all.

Australian government officials also state:

> Although commonly called the Tasmanian Tiger or Tasmanian Wolf, the thylacine has more in common with

its marsupial cousin the Tasmanian Devil. With a head like a wolf, striped body like a tiger and backward facing pouch like a wombat, the thylacine was as unbelievable as the platypus, which had caused disbelief and uproar in Europe when it was first described.

The thylacine looked like a long dog with stripes, a heavy stiff tail and a big head. A fully grown thylacine could measure one hundred and eight centimeters from the tip of the nose to the tip of the tail, stand fifty-eight centimeters high at the shoulder and weigh about thirty kilograms. It had short, soft fur that was brown except for the thick black stripes, which extended from the base of the tail to the shoulders.

Well, that's all very fascinating, but the Puerto Rican chupacabra is almost exclusively described as being a bipedal beast; it walks on two legs, not four. Surely a creature that looks like a wolf, and which gives the impression of a cross between a tiger and a kangaroo, couldn't walk on two legs as well as four … could it? Rather amazingly, yes, it actually could, and it did. It's time for a further examination of the Australian government's thylacine files:

The thylacine was said to have an awkward way of moving, trotting stiffly and not moving particularly quickly. They walked on their toes like a dog but could also move in a more unusual way—a bipedal hop. The animal would stand upright with its front legs in the air, resting its hind legs on the ground and using its tail as a support, exactly the way a kangaroo does. Thylacines had been known to hop for short distances in this position.

From Extinction to Resurrection

All of this brings us right back to Ed's weird words. Let's begin with his supposed place of work, the Dugway Proving Ground. In February 1942, President Franklin D. Roosevelt signed a piece of legislation that gave what was then called the War Department complete jurisdiction over more than one hundred and twenty thousand acres of land in Utah. It wasn't long before the DPG was up and running. And it's still doing exactly that today, but now with the benefit of almost three-quarters of a million acres of heavily guarded and near-inaccessible land. The best way to describe the base is as an Area 51 that, instead of allegedly researching crashed UFOs and autopsying dead aliens, focuses its top-secret research on deadly viruses and exotic diseases, those pesky things that usually provoke catastrophic zombie outbreaks in the likes of *The Walking Dead* and *Night of the Living Dead*.

As our e-mail exchange progressed, Ed opened up, and significantly so, too. He claimed that back in the 1980s staff at the Dugway Proving Ground got its hands on thylacine DNA and secretly decided to try and resurrect the creature from the clutches of the Grim Reaper, Lazarus-style. High-tech gene-splicing and cloning were reportedly the order of the day. According to Ed, it all worked very well. The beast, both incredibly and amazingly, walked—and hopped—yet again. Not in Australia, New Guinea, or Tasmania, but right in the heart of Mormon country.

As for why the creature was resurrected, this is where it all got really controversial. According to Ed, the military wanted to create an army of savage beasts that could be unleashed on the battlefield and tear the enemy apart, rather than take them out with conventional bullets and the like. The thylacine was seen as the perfect beast, chiefly because of its immense, powerful jaws. There was something else, however. Mad scientists at the proving ground had created a terrible virus that plunged the infected into manic states of homicidal rage, which was very much the scenario in the *28 Days Later* and *28 Weeks Later* movies, which I referred to in an earlier chapter in relation to a somewhat similar scenario involving mutated monkeys in Puerto Rico. Those same scientists weren't using their nightmarish virus on people, however. The targets of experimentation were those resurrected thylacines, as if you couldn't guess. But long before the animals could be let loose in war zones, test runs had to be undertaken to see how catastrophically these creatures infected with a mind-altering virus really would behave. And which place was chosen for the tests? Yep: Puerto Rico.

A pack of frenzied, resurrected thylacines causing mayhem and havoc in Puerto Rico, and responsible for spawning the legend of the chupacabra: is that really what happened? It was hard to say. Ed assured me that he was speaking one hundred percent truth. He was even careful to comment on the fact that, as the Australian government confirmed, the thylacine had the extraordinary ability to walk like a wolf at one moment and then in a fashion akin to "a bipedal hop" in the next instant. This was why, Ed assured me, some people claimed the chupacabra appeared to resemble a large dog, and others said it walked on two legs. That the thylacine could walk in both fashions was the clincher, he said. Admittedly, that did make a certain degree of sense. And on that same specific matter, I'm going to now make a slight diversion to Russia, after which I'll return to Ed.

The Chupacabra Spreads Its (Bat-like) Wings

In April 2006, Russia's *Pravda* newspaper told a story that strongly suggested the chupacabra had somehow made its way to the heart of the former Soviet Union. It was a story that, to me, when I dug it out of my old files, suggested there just might be some merit to Ed's controversial claims:

> The worries began at the end of March 2005 not far
> from the regional center of Saraktash. On the Sapreka
> farm two farming families suddenly lost thirty-two tur-
> keys. The bodies of the birds, found in the morning, had
> been completely drained of blood. None of the farmers
> either saw or heard the beast that killed them. Then in
> the village of Gavrilovka sheep fell victim to the night-
> time vampire. The unknown animal was also in the
> hamlets of Vozdvizhenka and Shishma. In the course
> of the night three to four sheep or goats perished. All
> together the losses in the region amounted to thirty
> small horned cattle.

A farmer named Erbulat Isbasov, *Pravda* recorded, got a close look at the creature that was slaughtering his animals: "I heard the sheep start to bleat loudly. I run up to them and see a black shadow. It looked like an enormous dog that had stood up on its hind legs. And jumped like a kangaroo. The beast sensed my presence and ran away. It squeezed through an opening in the panels of the fence."

Although I kept a careful watch on this particular story, it soon died and the killings in Saraktash ended as mysteriously as they had begun. I have to say, though, that the references to "an enormous dog that had stood up on its hind legs" and which "jumped like a kangaroo" sounded astonishingly like the physical characteristics of a thylacine.

"A Creature We Were Not Supposed to See Has Escaped from a Secret Defense Lab"

August 2012 saw a dramatic development in the Russian chupacabra saga when a creature astonishingly like so many found across Texas popped up in another part of the former Soviet Union, specifically in Ukraine. It was canid, its limbs were disproportionate, and it was hairless. It would have looked perfectly at home on the property of Devin McAnally or in Phylis Canion's freezer. Ukraine was a hell of a long way from Texas, however.

"The animal doesn't look like a fox or a wolf, or a raccoon," commented Mikhail Ilchenko, the deputy head of the district veterinary service in Mikhailovskoe. He added: "It cannot even be a marten. I have never seen such animal before. But, judging by the fangs, I can definitely say that it is a predator."

Interestingly, in no time at all rumors surfaced, specifically concerning the creature's origins, which closely mirrored what I had heard in both Puerto Rico and Texas. The U.K.'s *Daily Mail* newspaper noted claims had been made that "It could be a 'mutant' fox poisoned by radiation, while another theory was that it may be a hybrid originating from a Soviet plant conducting tests on animals relating to chemical or biological weapons development. 'A creature we were not supposed to see has escaped from a secret defense lab,' said one comment."

Alexander Korotya of the Zoological Museum of Zaporozhye National University stated to the press: "I cannot identify what kind of animal it is. For example, its canine teeth are similar to a fox, but smaller in size—like a marten. Yet a marten has a different type of skull. If to compare with an otter's head, then the ears are too small. It has a wide nose and a stretched muzzle. My opinion is that it's most likely a hybrid animal or a mutant."

And now, with Russian conspiracies out of the way, back to Ed...

Spiked or Striped

Ed also had an ingenious explanation for the row of spikes that numerous people have claimed run down the necks of so many chupacabras. Ed told me that many of these sightings were made at dusk or after the sun had completely set, ensuring that visual sightings of the creature were somewhat distorted. When people reported seeing spikes, Ed explained, they were really catching brief glimpses of the tiger-like stripes that did indeed feature prominently on the backs of thylacines. True or not, I thought it was a plausible explanation.

As for how the story ended, Ed said that the thylacines proved to be far too difficult to handle, that the virus made them completely uncontrollable, and that the project was abandoned around 1997. Trying to round up the animals was seen as way too dangerous, as it might have given the game away, suggested Ed. So they were left alone to kill, reproduce, and do whatever else it is that the average thylacine does on an average day in Puerto Rico. And it was all successfully hidden behind the veil of myth, legend, rumor, and lore of the chupacabra.

There's something else, too. Ed was quite the enigmatic whistleblower. I have a friend who—how shall I put this?—is what I might describe as being "very good with computers." He offered to take a look at Ed's e-mail address, which was a Safe-mail.net account. As anyone who knows anything about such things, Safe-mail is often used by those who wish to protect their real identities and locations; its base of operations is in Israel. Encryption and cyber-stealth are the name of the game. It turned out that Ed's e-mails were coming from Utah, in a fashion. In reality, the e-mails were merely being routed through Utah, via at least two other locations. One was in Maryland and the other was in Langley, Virginia. It happens that Maryland is home to the National Security Agency, while Langley, Virginia, is the place that the CIA calls home.

That didn't mean or prove anything, but it was, um, interesting…

After about four or five days, Ed's e-mails suddenly stopped. I found that interesting too. In fact, I found everything about the affair interesting. Deep Throat or deeply disturbed nut, I never did find out.

Part 4

HUNTING VAMPIRES

Chapter 21
SACRIFICE AND VAMPIRES

On each and every occasion that I have visited Puerto Rico, I have heard fragmentary accounts of a very controversial nature. They are tales to the effect that the island's chupacabra phenomenon has very little to do with real vampires and far more to do with something else, full-blown animal sacrifice on the part of local occultists. In essence, the tales told to me suggested the chupacabra phenomenon was created by (or, at the very least, exploited by) one or more cults that used the vampire legend as a cover to protect and hide their identities and their sacrificial rites and rituals. Stories like this, of disturbing animal sacrifice, have fascinated me since I was a child.

The centuries-old English village of Pelsall, West Midlands, England, where I grew up, is situated just a ten-minute drive from the equally old town of Great Wyrley. Back in October 1903, a young resident of Great Wyrley named George Edalji was famously arrested, tried, and found guilty of fatally slashing a number of horses that belonged to the owner of Plant Pit Meadow, a local colliery.

Despite a lack of hard evidence that Edalji was the real culprit, he received a sentence of seven years. He was, however, released in 1906, chiefly as a result of the combined efforts of R.D.
Yelverton, previously the Chief Justice in the Bahamas, and Sir
Arthur Conan Doyle, the creator of the world's most famous
fictional detective, Sherlock Holmes. Such was the strength of
Doyle's belief that Edalji was innocent, he even penned a book
on the affair, *The Story of Mr. George Edalji*. The story was well
known all around Great Wyrley and Pelsall, even in the late
1970s, when, in my pre-teen years, I first heard of it.

What I found particularly intriguing is that at the time the
horse attacks were at their height, there were rumors in the local
media they were nothing less than sacrificial offerings to "elder
gods." The Edalji family was originally from India and, despite
the fact that George's father, Shapurji, was the vicar of the town's
St. Mark's Parish Church, was most unfairly perceived as a pack
of sinister outsiders by many within Great Wyrley. It was this
undeniably racist attitude that collectively, and inevitably, had a
hand in George being branded as the attacker. Regardless of who
really was responsible, the 1903 attacks, when combined with
their close association to where I used to live, led me to take a
deep interest in tales of animal sacrifice in the modern era.

The Rhayader Beast

In 1988, I investigated a very weird spate of animal deaths in
mid-Wales. The location was the ancient town of Rhayader.
Over a period of approximately twelve weeks, the people of
the town were plunged into a collective state of terror. The reason was as simple as it was nightmarish: the town's sheep population was drastically cut back by a vicious predator that killed

the animals with a single, two-pronged bite. There was hushed talk among the locals of vampires, of blood-sucking abominations. There was, however, also talk of occult groups that were using the sheep in nighttime sacrificial rites to appease ancient deities.

Whatever the truth of the matter, the attacks came to an abrupt end in December 1988, and the mystery was never resolved in terms of actually proving who or what was responsible. A chupacabra-like monster in the wilds of Wales, or a band of worshippers of who knows what, doing their very best to make it look like the killings were the work of a deadly monster? Despite spending a few days in town, I never did find out the answer to that question.

Bringing a Legendary Vampire to Life

In 2003 I began digging very deeply into the strange world of one Major General Edward Lansdale and his ties to the world of the vampire. Lansdale was a man highly skilled in the field of what is known in military circles as psychological warfare. Back in the early 1950s, Lansdale, who rose to prominence during the Second World War while working with the Office of Strategic Services (a forerunner of the CIA), spread rumors throughout the Philippines that a deadly vampire was wildly on the loose. Its name was the Aswang, a blood-sucking monstrosity of which the people of the Philippines lived in complete dread. The reason for Lansdale's actions was as bizarre as it was simple.

At the time, specifically 1952, the Philippines were in turmoil and chaos as a result of an uprising by the Hukbalahap, or Huks, as they were also known. They were vehemently anti-government rebels and did their very best to oust the president of the Philippines, Elpidio Rivera Quirino, with whom Lansdale was friends. And when the major general was asked by Quirino to help end the reign of terror that the Hukbalahap had generated, he quickly came on board.

One of the first things that Lansdale noted was that the rebels were deathly afraid of the vampiric Aswang and its nocturnal blood-drinking activities. So he came up with a brainstorm, albeit a grisly one. It was a brainstorm that was kept secret for decades, until Lansdale himself finally went public, long after his prestigious military career was finally over. As the major general recalled:

> To the superstitious, the Huk battleground was a haunted place filled with ghosts and eerie creatures. A combat psywar squad was brought in. It planted stories among town residents of an Aswang living on the hill where the Huks were based. Two nights later, after giving the stories time to make their way up to the hill camp, the psywar squad set up an ambush along the trail used by the Huks.

That same psywar squad then did something that was very radical, but which proved to be extremely effective. They silently grabbed one of the Hukbalahap rebels, snapped his neck, and then, using a specially created metallic device, left two deep, vicious-looking puncture marks on the neck of the man. But that was barely the start of things. They then quietly tied a rope around the man's ankles, hung his body from a nearby tree, and let just about as much blood as possible drain out of the body. After several hours, the corpse was lowered to the ground and left close to the Hukbalahap camp, specifically to ensure it was found by his comrades. They found it.

The result, as Lansdale noted, was overwhelmingly positive, from the perspective of the Philippine government at least: "When the Huks returned to look for the missing man and found their bloodless comrade, every member of the patrol believed that the Aswang had got him and that one of them would be next if they remained on that hill. When daylight came, the whole Huk squadron moved out of the vicinity."

It was an ingenious and spectacularly successful tactic, one that was reportedly utilized on more than fifteen occasions to take back strategic ground from the Hukbalahap soldiers. A vampire of legend was now one of reality, or so the rebels believed. Is it feasible that the vampire of Puerto Rico had been similarly created—not to wage war, but to allow groups that practiced sacrificial rites to camouflage their activities behind tales of the chupacabra? The more I looked into the controversial theory, the more I came to realize that it was something that could not be discounted.

Chapter 22

THE MOCA VAMPIRE

If there's one thing more than any other that annoys me in the field of paranormal research, it's an armchair researcher of the debunking kind. Time and time again I have heard the debunkers loudly assert (often in high-pitched, whiny voices, and with their arms firmly folded) that the chupacabra simply cannot and does not exist. How do they know? Well, actually, they don't know. Have they personally visited Puerto Rico? For the most part, no, they have not. Have they sat down opposite a witness and actually spoken to them? Nope. Hardly more than the barest occasion. What they have done is to secure their data from that bastion of truth and reliability known as the Internet. Not a good sign, to say the least.

As to why the debunkers piss me off so much, it's not just as a result of their lazy approach and attitude. It's because by not actually visiting the places in question and speaking with the people on the ground, they are missing out on a wealth of untapped data that simply cannot be found by just opening Google and typing in the words, "Puerto Rico + chupacabra."

A perfect case in point: if the chupacabra is a real creature, ask the naysayers, then why did it suddenly surface out of nowhere in 1995? Well, actually, it didn't. Yes, it did, they reply; the Internet says so. Well, yes, the Internet does say that. But try speaking to the locals. When you gain their confidence and trust you quickly find yourself immersed in a very different story. This was something that became abundantly clear to me just one day into my first expedition to Puerto Rico, in the summer of 2004.

As well as a cameraman and director, our team comprised a sound guy and a couple of drivers, all of whom were native to the island. On day two, we stopped for lunch at a roadside café and I got chatting with the guys. As I did so, something remarkable surfaced. All of them laughed and scoffed at the idea that the chupacabra was a modern-day phenomenon. They pointed out that, yes, those emotive words chupacabra and goat sucker were relatively new. No one disputed that. They added, however, that blood-sucking monstrosities of vampire-like proportions had been reported across the island not just for years but for decades, at least since the 1970s. I could suggest that the saga of Frank Drake and the vampire of Puerto Rico's Arecibo Telescope pushes the boundaries back to at least the 1960s.

What separated the earlier reports from those of the 1990s and the 2000s, I was told, was that they had largely been forgotten or overlooked. Plus, it was explained to me, the lack of the Internet back then meant that, just like Las Vegas, whatever happened in Puerto Rico largely stayed there. A perfect case in point, they said, was a beast that became known as the Moca Vampire.

History and Mystery

Noted for its fruit industry and cattle farming, Moca is a cool place, filled with old and atmospheric buildings and surrounded by amazing forestland and green hills. Back in the mid-1970s, the municipality was home to something else, too: the Moca Vampire. It was a most apt title for a creature that caused brief havoc and mayhem in March 1975. Pigs, goats, chickens, geese, cattle, and even pets were found violently slaughtered, specifically in the Barrio Rocha suburb of Moca. I know this since the guys on the crew, as well as numerous locals in Moca itself, were happy to reveal all during the course of my first excursion to the island.

The lair of the bloody beasts.

The bodies of the dead animals were quickly collected by the authorities and were subjected to necropsy, which was said to have demonstrated that at least some of them had been drained of notable amounts of blood. The people of the area, hardly surprisingly, were plunged into states of fear and anxiety. Children were kept indoors at night. Armed police patrolled the streets after sunset. Matters came to a horrific climax when the monster turned its attention away from animals and towards the human population.

One of the most traumatic attacks occurred on March 25, when a woman was viciously clawed by what she described as a fearful-looking beast covered in feathers. Then another story surfaced. Utterly petrified by what occurred, the witness reported that late one night in March, a huge, winged monster landed on the zinc roof of her Moca home and let loose with an ear-splitting scream. She feared for her very life, as the mighty thing clanged around loudly in the darkness, only mere feet above her living room.

Just a couple of days later, a rancher in the area found more than thirty of his chickens dead, all slaughtered by a silent, stealthy killer. Overall, across a two-week period in March 1975, around ninety animals were killed and an untold number of Moca residents were living in downright terror. The monstrous affair was never resolved. Fortunately, however, the attacks stopped as mysteriously and as quickly as they had begun.

It should be noted that, as I was told by the guys on the TV shoot, a theory made the rounds at the time that occultists, rather than a deadly monster, were the cause of the attacks; occultists whose activities revolved around sacrificial blood rites, for which the tale of the Moca Vampire offered convenient and ingenious cover. This was not the only time a story reached my ears to the effect that the assumed attacks of the bloodsuckers of Puerto Rico were actually the creation of those that engaged in rite, ritual, and sacrifice.

Chapter 23

THE VILLAGE OF THE UNDEAD

Sometimes an investigation will take the average adventurer in a direction very different to that originally anticipated. Exactly that happened to Jon Downes and me when we were in Puerto Rico in 2004. We found ourselves plunged into a deeply weird story of nothing less than a third breed of island vampire. The chupacabra and the vampire of Moca, it seemed, had a rival in the blood-drinking stakes.

Puerto Rico is a place filled to the brim with dark superstitions, with beliefs in all manner of paranormal phenomena, and with an acceptance that terrible and savage things lurk deep within the woods and forests. I'm inclined to think they do live there! One such story that really caught our attention, on day five, was focused on the alleged existence of an isolated village somewhere on the Rio Canovanas (in English, the Canovanas River). It's a river that dominates the municipality of Canovanas, in the northeast of Puerto Rico, and that is noted for its green hills and extensive plains.

According to the tale, which half the film crew and a couple of locals had all heard, the entire population of the village was afflicted by a strange malady—a very strange malady. The village folk, we were told, were skinny, pale, and downright anemic looking. They never surfaced during daylight hours. They only ever dressed in black. And here was the clincher: they fed on nothing but fresh blood. To a pair of English vampire hunters, it all sounded great; it was precisely the sort of thing Jon and I were looking for. That didn't mean it was true, however. Or did it? Well, let's see.

It has been my experience that behind just about every controversial legend or rumor there is usually a nugget or several of truth, even if it is somewhat distorted. We asked our storytellers to expand on what they knew of this infernal tribe of bloodsuckers. They were happy to do so. The picture their words painted was notably unsettling.

A Close Encounter of the Viral Kind

None of the people of the village exceeded four-and-a-half feet in height, we were told. Their heads were larger than normal and were marked with prominent, blue veins. They were completely lacking in hair. Some of them had nothing less than six fingers on each hand. Their noses were almost beak-like. They had skin that gave them a leathery, wrinkled, aged look. Their genitals were supposedly nearly nonexistent. As for their voices, they were oddly high-pitched. They walked with a stiff, robotic gait. And they dined voraciously on human blood.

On hearing all of this, Jon and I looked knowingly at each other. The symptoms that were described to us (aside, that is, from the blood drinking) were not those of vampirism at all, but of a distressing and extremely rare condition called progeria—a tragic genetic affliction that affects children. In fact, it's so rare that, officially at least, only one case exists per every eight million people on the planet. Progeria provokes rapid aging and a physical appearance nearly identical to that of the so-called vampires that dwelled on the Canovanas River. In some cases, those with progeria show signs of polydactylism—an extra digit on the hands and / or feet. Life spans are usually short, from early teens to (at the absolute extreme) the twenties.

Of course, given the rarity of progeria, this instantly made both of us wonder how was it possible that an entire village could be affected by this genetic disorder, across what we were told were at least several generations? The answer we got was as amazing as it was controversial.

Back in 1957, something was said to have crashed to earth in the Canovanas region, something very unusual, as I mentioned in an earlier chapter. Among those we spoke to, opinion was split between a meteorite and a craft from another world—a UFO. Whatever the culprit, it had let loose a strange alien virus, one that wormed its way into the water supply of the village and, in no time at all, infected the population of thirty or forty. The result was disastrous; each and every subsequent newborn displayed the awful symptoms of what to Jon and me sounded acutely like progeria.

As startling as it may seem, the threat of an alien virus surfacing on our world is one that NASA takes very seriously.

"Harmful Contamination"

According to the text of Article IX of The Treaty on Principles Governing the Activities of States in the Exploration and Use of Outer Space, Including the Moon and Other Celestial Bodies that was collectively signed at Washington, D.C., London, England,

and Moscow, Russia on January 27, 1967, and entered into force on October 10 of that year:

> In the exploration and use of outer space, including the Moon and other celestial bodies, States Parties to the Treaty shall be guided by the principle of co-operation and mutual assistance and shall conduct all their activities in outer space, including the Moon and other celestial bodies, with due regard to the corresponding interests of all other States Parties to the Treaty.

Most significant of all is the next section of the document:

> States Parties to the Treaty shall pursue studies of outer space, including the Moon and other celestial bodies, and conduct exploration of them so as to avoid their harmful contamination and also adverse changes in the environment of the Earth resulting from the introduction of extraterrestrial matter and, where necessary, shall adopt appropriate measures for this purpose.

It must be stressed that the main concern, as described in the document, revolved around the fear that a deadly virus would be released into the Earth's atmosphere, a worldwide pandemic would begin, and an unstoppable plague would escalate, ultimately killing each and every one of us. But what if that same alien pandemic didn't kill us, but instead provoked progeria-style symptoms and a craving for human blood?

Extraterrestrial Parallels

Such a possibility sounds manifestly unlikely in the extreme. It's worth noting, however, that the so-called extraterrestrial "Grays" of "alien abduction" lore—those dwarfish, skinny, black-eyed, and gray-skinned creatures that are so instantly recognizable to one and all and made famous on the likes of *The X-Files*—do, admittedly, display far more than a few characteristics of progeria.

On the matter of the Grays possibly being affected by progeria, *Flying Saucer Review* magazine noted:

If Grays have progeria, then there is a very serious situation out there. An entire civilization may be threatened with extinction because their children and young people are dying. A possible reason why progeria may be so widespread among Grays and not among humans is probably because the Grays have been around much longer than humans and the DNA replication is probably deteriorating, making room for genetic mutations and serious genetic diseases … One reason why they may want to hybridize with *Homo sapiens* is to add healthier DNA to their gene pool and to weed out the progeria gene.

I chatted with Jon about this and I had to wonder, was it feasible that a strange, extraterrestrial plague—or, perhaps, futuristic gene-tinkering linked to the alien abduction phenomenon—had provoked a disastrous outbreak of something that manifested in a combination of progeria and vampirism, all among the population of a small Puerto Rican village?

It seemed incredible and outlandish to even give the matter serious thought. Certainly, when all attempts to verify the story came to absolutely nothing, and even the exact location in question could not be identified, we came to a couple of tentative conclusions. First, perhaps what was being described was not progeria after all, but the results of decades of in-breeding in a village that was in dire need of new blood (no pun intended). Second, the idea that these unfortunate people were vampires was almost certainly born out of superstitious fear of their curious appearances, rather than hard, literal proof that they thrived on human blood, which they almost certainly did not.

Unfortunately, and regardless of the truth of the matter, everything was against us in this investigation. No one was able to point us in the specific direction of the village. To the best of everyone's knowledge, no photographs of the villagers existed. And, the tight schedule we were on meant that there simply wasn't time to pursue this admittedly fascinating tale.

While a down-to-earth explanation was probably the likely one, try as we might neither I nor Jon could fully dismiss from our minds the dark notion that Puerto Rico might harbor a band of unholy vampires of the outer space kind, a band with a voracious need for human blood. It was a chilling thought. It still is.

Chapter 24

BLOOD GETS SPILLED IN OLD SAN JUAN

The island of Puerto Rico is home to a number of different religions, one of them being Santeria, which is also practiced throughout much of the rest of the Caribbean. Its origins, however, can be found in the traditions of the Yoruba people of the Federal Republic of Nigeria, West Africa. While those who adhere to the teachings of Santeria believe in the existence of one overall god, they also believe there are numerous sub-gods too, which are collectively known as the Orishas. Those who are initiated into the religion are known as Santeros, and are required to go through a weeklong process of purification, one which involves the application of both herbs and water to carefully and completely cleanse the body.

Not only that, a great deal of time and effort is expended by the Santeros when it comes to the appeasement of their many and varied sub-deities. One way in which this has been achieved (but far less so today) is by animal sacrifice—specifically, the killing of chickens and goats, which just happen to be the most favored delicacies of the Puerto Rican vampire, as we have now seen time and time again.

In November 1992, three years before the chupacabra phenomenon took off big time, a major controversy surfaced in Florida, where Santeria has a significantly sized following. It's a following dominated by the Church of Lukumi Babalu Aye, which was created in 1974 by Oba Ernesto Pichardo. As a result, the city of Hialeah, in Miami-Dade County, passed a law banning the practice of animal sacrifice. In 1992, this law was challenged by the church, in the Supreme Court, no less. A sound and valid argument was made to the effect that preventing the followers of Santeria from carrying out a prime aspect of their traditions was unconstitutional. The argument proved to be convincing. On June 11, 1993, the church won the case.

Seeking the Santeros

In mid-2007, I was once again on the island with which I now had so much affinity. I decided that I would spend the four days at my disposal trying to get to the heart of the claims that at least some tales of the chupacabra and its deadly attacks on livestock might be the concoctions of groups that engaged in sacrificial activity. Since such rumors existed they at least had to be addressed.

Santeria has a long history in Puerto Rico. It took much of its inspiration from Nigerian slaves shipped over to the island in the eighteenth century. As for the matter of animal sacrifice, this was typically carried out by a Santero who was well versed in the many and varied intricacies of the religion. The reasons for such sacrifices were numerous and included a desire for physical well-being, riches, and good fortune. Like each and every paranormal pact, this one came at a price.

A Santero would rub the skin of a paying client with the body of the animal that was to be imminently sacrificed. Doing so transferred whatever ailed the person, or whatever they desired, into the body of the animal, or so the followers of Santeria believed. The sacrificing of the animal was an act designed to ensure the wish reached the Orishas, who granted them whatever it was that the person in question required. Sometimes the corpse of the animal was destroyed; on other occasions it was eaten. As for the blood, it was served in a large vessel and then offered to the gods.

Since Santeria has a large and acknowledged following in Puerto Rico (although it's important to note that the sacrificial angle, today, is largely symbolic rather than literal), it's most unlikely that its adherents would need to pass any sacrifices off as attacks undertaken by the chupacabra. There is, however, another group, allegedly, in Puerto Rico that might find it to its advantage to do exactly that.

Uncovering Secrets in Old San Juan

Santeria has an offshoot known variously as Mayombe, Palo, or Palo Mayombe, but which for the sake of ease I will refer to as Palo. Its rituals, which supposedly grant wealth, health, and power, are essentially identical to those of regular Santeria. But not always. While in Puerto Rico in May 2007 I was able to hook up with a man named Sal, who knew a great deal about the dark world of Palo and who told me a profoundly disturbing story.

It was around 7:00 p.m. on a bustling, hot Friday evening and we were hanging out in a run-down, darkened bar in Old San Juan's La Perla district. It's an area that even many of the locals choose to avoid at night. Major drug deals, smuggling, and arms trafficking are rife throughout the district after sunset.

Even the cops, whenever possible, prefer to leave things well alone in La Perla. I thought it was a pretty cool place.

The bar was one where salsa music endlessly blasted out of the speakers, where it was wise to keep one eye on your cash and credit cards, and the other on your back, and where even making a trip to the bathroom was potentially hazardous. Scowling, narrowed eyes followed me as, halfway through the evening and filled to the brim with tequila, I responded to a call of nature. The trick was not to be fazed or intimidated. If you succumbed, you were probably doomed to end your days in a dark back-alley, just mere moments after leaving the bar. Fortunately, I grew up on the outskirts of Birmingham, England, where one learns very quickly the importance of knowing how to look after oneself late on a Friday night and in the heart of a big city. That was why, when Sal and I entered the bar, I quickly figured that the best place for us to sit was at a table that provided a full view of the room and which was right next to a side door, just in case a rapid exit was needed.

Sacrifices of the Rich and Famous

Sal, thirty-something, dark-haired, and jowly, worked in a local restaurant. As I sat and listened, he told me a number of stories that had come to him secondhand by what he described as a friend in the butcher trade. Admittedly, I wasn't altogether happy about relying on a story that came from a friend of a friend (and maybe of yet another friend too), but in this case, I really had no choice.

Sal said there existed in Puerto Rico what can only be described as a rogue form of Palo, one that was far removed from its conventional, original form and which practiced highly controversial rituals. The group, he added, was one that pretty much no one in the regular Santeria community knew about or was linked to. The rituals of the group typically revolved around the sacrifice of chickens, goats, and peacocks. According to Sal, the group began its deadly activities in late 1994 or maybe early 1995 and was focused on providing a unique service: a guarantee of power and wealth in return for a great deal of money.

This was, without doubt, very similar to the world of the Santeros, except for one thing. Sal said that many of the people who had sold their souls to this Palo offshoot were nothing less than major household names and included famous actors, politicians, musicians, authors, and even, he claimed, certain figures in the world of royalty.

Some of the rituals, Sal said, were held in a large and spacious house, one that was owned by a rich and influential figure in the equally rich and influential area of Condado, which is situated in Santurce, a district of San Juan. Other rituals were supposedly undertaken, in somewhat dicey fashion, deep in the heart of the El Yunque rain forest. As well as sacrifices and the dishing up of dead bodies to ancient deities, wild alcohol- and cocaine-fueled orgies were the name of the game too. It all reminded me of something straight out of the Tom Cruise and Nicole Kidman movie *Eyes Wide Shut*. I distinctly remember thinking at the time that I sincerely hoped Sal hadn't made all this up after seeing and getting over-excited by the movie.

As for the chupacabra connection to the story, Sal claimed that while the group was not responsible per se for creating the legend of the beast, the members most definitely exploited it to their great advantage and to the absolute hilt. By that, he meant, particularly in relation to the events in El Yunque, when the group was busy killing chickens and goats in the rain forest, and then draining their blood and offering it up to the gods, it made a great deal of sense for them to spread tales of a chupacabra or several on the loose. By doing so, their controversial actions remained buried under a mass of tales of an animal-killing, blood-drinking creature that might not actually exist or that actually might.

The territory of the chupacabra.

Could Sal help me to track down the group? Nope. Could he give me its name? Not a chance. Was there anything else he could tell me? Not a thing, aside from the fact that those who practiced regular Santeria were not the culprits. The group he was talking about was something else entirely. It was very much just a case of "here's what I know; take it or leave it." I decided, on balance, to choose the former. Sal's story proved nothing. It did, however, strongly suggest to me that the truth behind the chupacabra legend was far more complex and confusing than most observers of the phenomenon had ever realized.

We finished our tequila and headed out into the swarming streets of La Perla. The air was hot, sticky, and dominated by the odors of human sweat, cigars, perfume, and meat roasting somewhere nearby. I grabbed a cab back to my San Juan hotel. With a wave of his hand, Sal vanished amid the huge throng of Friday night partiers.

Santeria in San Antonio

One final thing on this matter: I have not found any evidence to suggest that practitioners of Santeria have ever used the chupacabra phenomenon as a cover to undertake their controversial rituals in Texas. Nor have I uncovered any evidence of such actions undertaken by a rogue element of Santeria, of the kind that Sal referred to and claimed knowledge of. Ken Gerhard, however, did make an interesting and relevant observation to me on this matter in 2014:

> Since I moved to San Antonio, about eight years ago, I've heard many references to people practicing voodoo-like, ritualistic religions throughout San Antonio. It's a very traditional city, with Mexican and American heritage. I do know a gentleman who was in charge of cleaning out abandoned houses and he claims—he told me—that he was in the process of cleaning out one abandoned house when he went down to the basement. He found this really weird, Santeria-like altar, where they had little voodoo dolls nailed to boards and strange symbols.

It's worth noting, too, that there are other examples of Santeria-based animal sacrifice in the Lone Star State.

"The Greater Houston Area
Is Home to Thousands of Santeria Believers"

In 2009, a man named Jose Merced, a Santeria priest, sued the Texas city of Euless for prohibiting him from sacrificing goats in ceremonial fashion. Merced, interestingly, was originally from Puerto Rico; he argued that it was his religious freedom to do what he wanted, where he wanted, and when he wanted. The court concluded otherwise, based upon the city's stance that Merced's actions could affect public health and might contravene city laws and legislation surrounding the slaughtering of animals. When it was shown that Merced had dumped the remains of sacrificed chickens into a local stream, his case against Euless was thrown out of court. But that wasn't the end of the controversy. In October 2009, the U.S. Fifth Circuit Court of Appeals found in Merced's favor. The sacrifices continued after all.

In February 2014, the *Houston Chronicle* profiled the life and work of a Santeria priestess named Faizah Perry. The newspaper noted: "Perry estimates the greater Houston area is home to thousands of Santeria believers."

I knew that none of this conclusively proved disciples of a Santeria-like offshoot were using the relatively recent rise of the chupacabra in Texas as a means to get around city laws and slaughter goats, chickens, and who knew what else. But I thought, and I still think, that it's intriguing Santeria and sacrifice is practiced in two places noted for heavy concentrations of animal killings attributed to the chupacabra: Puerto Rico and Texas.

Part 5

HOAXES AND
MISTAKEN IDENTITY

Chapter 25

"IT'S ALIVE!!"

On one particular morning in late 2004, I received a phone call from an elderly man who had seen the SyFy Channel's show on my quest, with Jon Downes, to solve the riddle of the Puerto Rican chupacabra. Unlike a lot of authors, I'm totally fine with my e-mail address appearing online and my phone number appearing in the phone book, which is almost certainly why I get so many calls and e-mails, some good, some bad, and some downright insane. The man in question wanted to do more than just have a casual chat, however: he claimed to have a chupacabra in his backyard. Yes, you did read that right. Well, that's certainly not the kind of thing you hear every day! The caller was a resident of Grapevine, only about a forty minute drive from where I lived at the time. You won't be surprised to know that I offered to come and take a careful and close look at the body—as in right now.

The man quickly corrected me: "No, it's not a body. It's not dead. It's in a trap. It's alive."

This, to be sure, was a major development. As I work from home, it was not a problem to check out the deadly monster for myself. "I can be there within an hour," I told the man.

That would work, he replied. I grabbed a rucksack, one that is always packed with a camera, audio equipment, and a camcorder, fueled up the car, and got on the road. It was time to finally confront, face to face, what was rapidly becoming my very own monstrous nemesis.

The Scene of the Animalistic Action

Ten minutes before I arrived, I called the guy on my cell to let him know I was almost there. As a result, when I pulled up he was already on the front yard, pacing around in a vest and shorts. I got out of the car and a creature suddenly charged me. No, it wasn't a chupacabra: it was a small dachshund, not at all happy to see his personal territory invaded by a stranger with an even stranger non-Texan accent. The white-haired man, Ray, called his dog off my ankle. We shook hands and walked inside Ray's home. I was offered a very welcome tall glass of iced lemonade and we cut straight to the chase.

It's important that, first, I tell you a little bit about the location. Although Ray's home was built on a regular, suburban street, it backed onto a stretch of woodland that, while not large, was certainly densely packed. As we sat in the living room Ray told me that for several nights previously his little dog, Fuzz, had constantly wanted outside. In fact, the dog had practically tried to scratch the backdoor down. Aware that something wild was likely out there, lurking in the shadows, Ray scooped up Fuzz in his hands and took a few tentative steps outside. He saw nothing, but he did hear a furious scuffle somewhere near the line of the fence. So did Fuzz who, in Ray's own immortal words, which I still remember to this day, went "plum goofy."

Late on the next night, however, Ray caught sight of a pale-looking animal that was not overly large, but that clearly reacted to his and the dog's presence on the back porch. That's to say it shot off into the darkness and quickly vanished. Ray was determined to figure out what the beast was, and borrowed from a hunter friend a steel trap-style cage, one with a pressure activated dropdown door. Late on the following afternoon, Ray placed various items of food and a bowl of water in the trap. He positioned it near the fence, which was overlooked by the woods. And then he waited, patiently but excitedly. Although he heard nothing untoward that night, when he went out to check on the trap the next morning, Ray got the absolute shock of his life: a bizarre creature was sitting in the cage, staring right at him. Skinny, hairless and with penetrating eyes, it made for a profoundly eerie sight.

At that point in the conversation, Ray asked me if I wanted to see it.

Of course, I did!

We walked to the backdoor. I was about to confront a real-life chupacabra.

I Meet a Monster. Well, No, Actually, I Don't

Sure enough, there was the creature, watching us carefully as we approached it. Its body was hairless. Its legs were noticeably long. Its head was long and pointed. Its ears stood up prominently. It had a fierce and determined look on its face. It was, unfortunately, a possum with mange. I knew exactly what a possum looked like, rather ironically, I had helped a neighbor capture no less than three possums under similar circumstances in the previous year. Granted, they weren't mangy, but I sure as hell knew what I was seeing and what I was not seeing.

When I told Ray what he had really caught, he replied, very defensively: "No, it's a chupacabra."

"No, it's a possum with mange," I repeated, firmly.

"No, it's a chupacabra."

"No … it's … a … possum," I said, again, this time slowly and deliberately.

Ad infinitum—almost.

Even though there was nothing remotely odd about the animal, aside from its hairless condition, which, admittedly, did make it look very weird, I asked Ray if I could take a photo of it. He hemmed and hawed and finally said "No." Not at all impressed by my down-to-earth explanation, he said he was going to contact one of the local television news stations and sell his own photos for a fistful of dollars.

I assured Ray that when the TV people brought in a wildlife expert, as they most surely would, the identification of the creature would be confirmed very quickly, and no one would be interested in the photos in the slightest. He again assured me it was a chupacabra, so yes, they would be interested—very interested. We were doing nothing but going around in circles. We shook hands, and I went on my way. Since Ray's story, and the attendant photos, never made it to the news, I figured that, just like me, Dallas's media wasn't buying into the chupacabra angle either.

Even though the animal Ray had snared was clearly not a chupacabra, the affair was still of great importance. Here's why: it demonstrated to me that such was the growing attraction of the chupacabra legend, just about any unusual looking animal could be offered up as the legendary sucker of goats. And was being offered up! As the years progressed, I found myself in more than a few very similar situations. Each and every case had one thing in common: they taught me to be very cautious of any and all claims of captured, killed, or caged chupacabra.

Chupie, RIP: Parallels with the Grapevine Affair

In March 2014, six years after film footage of a strange, hairless animal with a huge, pig-like snout was filmed in DeWitt County, Texas, by Deputy Brandon Riedel, the area was once again the target of chupacabra seekers. I followed this story closely, since in many ways it mirrored the 2004 events at Grapevine, Texas, that I investigated, which revolved around a captured animal that I was told was a chupacabra, but which was really a snared, mange-riddled possum, as you've just seen.

As for the March 2014 case, it came from Jackie and Bubba Strong of Ratcliffe, Texas. In no time it was all over the Internet. The perplexed pair spotted an odd-looking, hairless animal as it did nothing more menacing than munch on tasty corn in a tree. There was not a bit of sucked or spilled blood in sight. The Strongs decided the animal had to be captured, and it was. They gave their newly caged prisoner a name, Chupie. It was well looked after; the couple fed it more corn, supplemented with a solid supply of cat food. The story did not end well for Chupie, however, who was soon euthanized at a local animal shelter.

A game warden named Rex Mays opined to the Texas press that the animal was a raccoon with mange, which was almost certainly the case. The raccoon theory gained further support when footage taken by the Strongs showed the animal holding and eating its food with its paws. That it was captured after being seen in a tree is notable too, since trees are much-favored hangout places for raccoons. Nevertheless, the chupacabra-like overtones prompted Jackie and Bubba to plan to have poor, late lamented Chupie stuffed and forever immortalized in infamy.

Chapter 26

AN OUT-OF-PLACE PREDATOR

Cryptozoology is a distinctly multifaceted phenomenon. It encompasses hairy man-beasts, sea serpents, lake monsters, werewolves, Mothman, lizard people, and countless other bizarre and mysterious creatures, including the so-called "Alien Big Cat," or ABC, as it is generally known. For decades—in some countries for centuries—people have reported sightings of huge black cats roaming areas where, very simply, they should not exist.

In the United Kingdom, as a perfect example, each and every year dozens of reports surface about giant black cats prowling around the ancient landscape, slaughtering and devouring farm animals on a massive scale, with police marksmen dispatched to pump a hollow-tipped bullet or several into them, and with the local people seized by cold and unrelenting terror. Of course, the sensationalist British media loves it. It's much the same in Australia, which, just like the U.K., is not home to any kind of large, indigenous black cat. Yet the Aussies see such menacing creatures on a regular basis too, and they are clearly not spoiled, overfed housecats. So where are the ABCs coming from? The theories are intriguing. Definitive answers, however, are sorely lacking.

For some researchers of the ABC phenomenon, the big cats are probably the pets of people that purchased the animals illegally as cubs, and who found they couldn't look after them as they grew and grew, and so decided to secretly give them their freedom in the wild. There is a variation on this theme, one that is specifically relative to the U.K. It's a variation which suggests that when, in 1976, the British government modified the laws governing the keeping of big cats, many of the owners couldn't afford to pay the new highly inflated fees with which they were now faced. The result was that they stealthily released their animals into some of the larger forests of England, Wales, and Scotland by night, where there would be plenty of wild deer, rabbits, and foxes for the ABCs to live and thrive on.

What, you may be asking at this point, does all of this have to do with the chupacabra? Well, the answer is, depending on one's opinion, nothing, something, or just about everything. It's a little known fact that there are fragmentary stories of big cats hiding out in the more remote parts of Puerto Rico. Do you see where I'm going with this? I suspect that, yes, you do. Tales exist suggesting that, on more than a few occasions, an ABC has escaped into the wilds of Puerto Rico, gone on a voracious spree of killing and devouring just about anything and everything that crosses its path, and, in the process, has become an integral part of the chupacabra lore and legend.

Is it feasible that some of the attacks attributed to chupacabras might actually have their origins in the equally weird ABC phenomenon? It's a question that I can answer, at least, to a certain extent.

Fear Strikes Rio Piedras

My fifth foray into the world of the Puerto Rican vampire was in late December 2008. It turned out to be a profitable trip, but not in the way I had anticipated. Pretty much as soon as I arrived, I learned that one particular part of San Juan, Rio Piedras, was living in what could only be termed a state of downright fear. For more than three weeks, there had been sightings, exclusively at night, of a large black cat creeping around the neighborhood. Around four feet long and muscular, it was believed to have killed and eaten at least fifteen pet cats in the area, savaged a sheep or several, and apparently terrified a handful of people who crossed paths with it in the backstreets of Rio Piedras late on one particular Saturday night.

Local authorities took swift action. I know this for sure, as I took time out of my schedule to chat with a representative of the Department of Natural and Environmental Resources of Puerto Rico, specifically a spokesperson for the then secretary of the agency, Javier Velez Arocho. It was confirmed to me that an official file had been opened on the ABC encounters, that attempts had been made to humanely capture the beast, and that on three occasions live goats had been used to try and entice the cat to show itself, something that it was hoped would allow it to be tranquilized by the police. No luck: just like the ABCs everywhere, this one skillfully avoided all attempts to catch it or kill it.

Since my timing was fortuitous in the extreme, I decided to check out the area for myself. Dating back to the early part of the eighteenth century, Rio Piedras is most associated with students, because the district is home to the main campus of the large and impressive University of Puerto Rico. Despite being a student town, however, Rio Piedras does not have a particularly lively nightlife. Indeed, it's a fairly sedate part of San Juan, aside from when a marauding ABC is on the loose and causing chaos and getting misinterpreted as a chupacabra.

While most of the locals were reluctant to speak with me, which I have to say was slightly odd, I did strike gold while visiting the El Hipopotamo restaurant, located on Munoz Rivera Avenue. Serving local delicacies and fine wine, it had a relaxing, down-to-earth atmosphere. The good news was that the staff had heard all about the big cat reports, which is not surprising since the animal had been seen practically on their doorstep. When I told them why I was on the island, they were more than happy to chat with me.

It was most illuminating to learn there was talk in town of the ABC actually being a chupacabra. I asked why this was the case when the physical description of the creature—a large, sleek, black cat—was markedly different to that of the spiky-backed, bipedal, bat-winged thing of Puerto Rico. The answer was notable: the creature of Rio Piedras always attacked its victims by going for their throats and puncturing them with powerful teeth. Since that was the typical approach of the chupacabra, it was reasoned that the ABC was actually a deadly vampire. It became immediately evident to me that the staff didn't realize big cats typically go for the throat too.

This was a particularly important issue because it suggested people were less focused upon what the chupacabra looked like (or didn't), and were placing more emphasis on the nature of the attacks. In other words, for many, if an animal was found dead with puncture wounds to the neck, it had to have been the victim of a chupacabra attack, regardless of what others were maintaining about the appearance of the killer.

I also found it interesting that some of the employees had heard stories to the effect that the ABC was not a flesh and blood animal, but something of supernatural proportions. I had come across such things before—and on numerous occasions too. Certainly, the British big cats are perceived by some researchers as having nothing less than paranormal origins. In 2006, ABC authority Merrily Harpur wrote an entire book on that very angle, *Mystery Big Cats*. It was a book that was praised in some quarters and denounced as near-heresy by some of the more tedious, closed-minded characters in the ABC community.

An equally thought-provoking theory offered to me at the restaurant was that the Alien Big Cat of Rio Piedras was the escaped pet, or "mascot," of a local cocaine baron. It is a fact that drug lord types are not at all uncommon in Puerto Rico. Some of them, I was quietly advised, kept big cats as status symbols. I was, however, advised not to go looking for them: "It would not be good for you, sir," said my waitress, who, I deduced from the genuinely concerned look on her face, knew far more about such matters than she was willing to reveal.

I decided to ignore her words. After all, although Jon Downes and I had almost fallen foul of a dangerous gang back in 2004, we lived to tell to the tale. So what harm could a bit of nosing around of the druggy kind do me?

I Fought the Law

Getting the good folk of San Juan to spill the beans on local coke lords proved to be even more taxing than having them comment on the ABC/chupacabra mix-up that had almost turned certain parts of Rio Pedras into definitive no-go areas. Faced with the proverbial brick wall, I checked in with the Puerto Rican police (La Uniformada, or The Uniformed, as they are known) at their headquarters on San Juan's Franklin D. Roosevelt Avenue. They were very interested to know why, precisely, I was asking questions about coke dealers and big cats.

Only minutes after entering the building, I was "invited" to accompany the responding officer into an interview room, where I was told, rather than asked, to sit down. I was then met by an unsmiling captain with the Drugs Division, who asked for some identification. Shit. In mere moments, things had turned decidedly grim. I put my cards (and my driver's license) on the table and explained that I was looking into the theory that some reports of chupacabra attacks might have less to do with anything of a vampire nature and much more to do with coke and huge, marauding cats.

The captain looked at me with a face that overflowed with skepticism, almost to the point where I suspected he thought I was in cahoots with certain circulators of all things white, powdery, and nose destroying. That is, until I pulled out of my rucksack one of my older books on cryptozoology, which confirmed my "credentials" as someone who traveled the world in search of monsters. Or as the mustachioed captain no doubt perceived me: a certifiable, time-wasting nut.

I half expected him to take out his pistol and tell me to get my ass out of town by sunset or else, while the soundtrack to a Clint Eastwood–style western movie played in the background. But that was not the case at all. Satisfied that I was exactly who I claimed to be, the captain told me all that he knew about the chupacabra, which was basically just what had appeared in the press, chiefly back in the 1990s. As for the reports of big cats in Puerto Rico, he knew nothing concrete, but admitted to having heard a solitary story of an escaped jaguar. It was apparently seen by hikers on Cerro de Punta Mountain, four thousand, three hundred and ninety feet high, in Ponce, in the early 2000s. It was a story that was never resolved, since it was not investigated to anything beyond a cursory degree. That aside, there was nothing.

I stood up, we shook hands, and I left the building. About twenty feet outside of the door I turned around. The eyes of the arms-folded captain were intently focused on me. I waved and nodded. He returned neither the wave nor the nod. It's probably not a coincidence that when, two days later, I flew out of Luis Munoz Marin International Airport, my bags were vigorously searched before I took to the skies. Thankfully, the rubber gloves did not put in an appearance.

To this day, I'm not sure what to make of the Alien Big Cat connection (or non-connection) to the chupacabra mystery. What I can say for sure, however, is that I came across more than a few examples of people leaping to the conclusion that savage attacks to the throats of animals meant that a deadly chupacabra had to have been the culprit. Well, no, actually. As the above affair demonstrates, there are more than a few savage beasts roaming Puerto Rico, at least one of which took down its prey in a fashion not wholly dissimilar to the reported predations of the goat sucker. It was, and still is, an important thing to remember.

Chapter 27

MISTAKING BIGFOOT FOR THE CHUPACABRA!!

It's a little-known fact that the chupacabra is not the only weird beast rumored to haunt the island of Puerto Rico. Although certainly not on every occasion, but during at least two excursions to the island, I have uncovered fragmentary reports and accounts of encounters with what can only be described as Bigfoot-style creatures, as amazing or as unlikely as such a thing might sound. Without doubt, the most fascinating body of data on this curious issue came my way in 2013.

It's important I note from the very outset that many might think that talking about the Puerto Rican Bigfoot in a book about the island's chupacabra is far too much of a stretch to make a connection. In reality, the exact opposite is the case. As will become apparent very soon, the connection is all too real and ripe for scrutiny and comment. It revolves around two things: mistaken identity and the controversial, supernatural, phenomenon of shape-shifting. That's right—the chupacabra and the Bigfoot of Puerto Rico, according to some, at least, may be one and the same—which is why I feel it's an important story to tell. But before we get to that thorny matter, a bit of background as to why exactly I was yet again on the island.

It was August 1, 2013, and I was there to make a show with Galafilm Productions of Canada. It was titled *Mysteries at the National Parks*. The premise was an intriguing and original one; each and every episode of the series would focus its attention upon a paranormal mystery tied to a specific U.S. national park. And since Puerto Rico's El Yunque National Forest is the only rain forest in the entire United States National Forest System (USNFS), the plan was to make a show that focused on its infamous resident vampire.

To say that this trip was a brief one is an understatement. I flew out of Dallas-Fort Worth International Airport early on the morning of July 31, caught (with barely minutes to spare) a connecting flight in Florida, arrived at my San Juan hotel around 8:00 p.m., was filmed during a downpour of epic proportions in the heart of El Yunque the following morning, exited the rain forest around noon, and flew back to my Arlington, Texas, home around 7:30 p.m. that night. In between the end of the filming and the time of my departure, however, I had the good fortune to conduct an interview with a guy whose theories pushed the chupacabra mystery down previously uncharted pathways. They were pathways dominated by nothing less than the world's most infamous hairy wild man, Bigfoot.

A rainy day in Puerto Rico, as I seek out the
chupacabra-Bigfoot connection.

I have to say, although I was in Puerto Rico looking for the deadly sucker of goats and of other equally unfortunate animals, it was a welcome and refreshing diversion to find myself on the receiving end of something totally different. Peter was primarily a ghost hunter and paranormal investigator, also there to be filmed for the world of on-screen entertainment. Originally from Berlin, Germany, he had moved to Puerto Rico in 1996. Peter was someone whose accounts of Bigfoot activity in Puerto Rico were as fascinating as they were controversial. By that, I mean the reports had far less to do with what one might call unknown animals, and far more to do with what might justifiably be termed downright paranormal anomalies.

Opening Up the Bigfoot Files

It's important, at the very outset, that I stress Peter was not someone whose files on Bigfoot in Puerto Rico were overflowing. In fact, quite the opposite was the case. The number of reports in his archives was less than twenty and they spanned the mid-1970s to 1998, with a spate of reports dating from 1985. Typically, the beasts closely resembled the North American Bigfoot. That's to say they were large, humanoid, covered in dark hair, and solitary. While most of the reports emanated from or around the island's huge El Yunque rain forest, two were, rather incredibly, reported from the fringes of Puerto Rico's capital city, San Juan.

But Peter's Puerto Rican reports were filled with anomalies. He explained to me, as we chatted in the pleasant confines of the St. Germain Bistro and Café in Old San Juan, there were reports of the Puerto Rican Bigfoot seen in conjunction with anomalous lights in the sky, although not structured flying saucers, it must be noted. And, by in conjunction, I mean both time-wise and location-wise.

There were also reports of the creatures seemingly being impervious to bullets, which is an often-reported, curious aspect of North American cases. Certainly, the most controversial cases of which, Peter only had three examples, were of the creatures seemingly vanishing into nothingness.

Again, that "here one minute and gone the next minute" angle of the Bigfoot mystery is not unknown in the United States, even though many researchers of the phenomenon much prefer to ignore such hard-to-define cases. I, however, do not ignore them. In fact, I do the exact opposite: I embrace them. And there was something else too—something amazingly weird—even by my standards.

Peter had come to the conclusion, based on two specific reports, that the Puerto Rican Bigfoot and our old friend the chupacabra were one and the same. How could such a thing be? Well, by engaging in a bit of shape-shifting, that's how; something which cropped up in a 2010 chupacabra affair in Tecum-seh, Oklahoma, as discussed earlier in the pages of this book.

A Shift in Reality

Throughout history, folklore, and mythology, one can find ac-counts of terrible shape-shifting creatures, with the most fa-mous example surely being the werewolf. The deadly, savage monster of the full moon is far from being a unique entity, however. In Africa, there are legends of werehyenas. Wererats have been reported in the United States, chiefly in Oregon. Cy-nanthropy is a condition in which a person believes they can shape shift into the form of a dog. And then there are werecats.

Tales of werecats exist in numerous locations, including South America, Asia, Africa, and Europe. Sometimes the were-cats are nothing less than transformed humans. Leopards, lions, tigers, and jaguars are typically the werecat forms into which a human shape-shifter mutates. Others are regular cats, altered by dark magic into something hostile and infernal. All of which brings us back to the chupacabra.

As I was back in San Juan by 1:30 p.m. and didn't have to be at the airport until 5:00 p.m., I took my time listening carefully to what Peter had to say. Both cases were eerily and chillingly simi-lar, even though they took place in distinctly different timeframes and locales. The first had occurred in Ponce in 1977 and the sec-ond in Moca in 1983, the latter, of course, noted for the Moca Vampire saga of the mid-1970s. In both cases, the witnesses en-countered extremely tall, hairy, man-like entities that dropped to all fours when sighted, and which then, amazingly … began to change.

As the terrified witnesses looked on, the huge, bulky beasts significantly shrunk in size, their limbs became dog-like, and, here was the clincher, a row of sharp, spiked protrusions suddenly burst through the muscular backs of the animals. In both cases, the now-chupacabra-looking beasts offered nothing but a hostile snarl and a deep growl and bounded off into the safety of the thick surrounding trees. But that was not the end of things.

In the encounter at Ponce, the frightened witness, a woman named Gabriela, experienced something else too, something that in many respects was even stranger than seeing a Bigfoot shapeshift into a spiky, chupacabra-like monstrosity.

Gabriela, at the time of her sighting, was in a wooded area that overlooked Ponce, one she knew very well. Bafflingly, although Gabriela was able to keep her hometown in sight at all times as she fled the scene, Peter told me that Gabriela repeatedly found herself racing around in circles, in a state of confusion. It was as if the familiar landscape had somehow changed into something deeply unfamiliar, something malignant and horrific, something that was not going to allow her to leave. On top of that, an overwhelming, vacuum-like silence blanketed the entire environment. Fright became unbridled terror, as Gabriela realized that she was trapped, utterly unable to escape the woods. That is, for around fifteen minutes.

Suddenly, the strange, surreal atmosphere changed. Background noise flooded Gabriela's ears, her sense of direction returned, the feelings of panic and fear rapidly subsided, and in less than twenty minutes she was back in the heart of civilization, doing her utmost to calm down.

Going Around in Circles

I have to say that I found Peter's story fascinating. Why? Simple. I had heard such near-confounding things before. The British Isles, from where I originally hail, are filled with centuries-old stories of goblins, pixies, piskies, fairies, and brownies. We are talking, collectively, about the wee folk, the little people, magical entities that existed, and perhaps still exist, on the fringes of what we call "reality." Not only were these diminutive entities shape-shifters, they also possessed the ability to place humans into a strange state of mind, one that centuries ago was referred to in whispered tones as "pisky-led."

In her 1890 book *Cornish Feasts and Folk-lore*, author Margaret Ann Courtney said of these diminutive, "elemental" entities that: "When mischievously inclined, pisky often leads benighted people a sad dance; like Will of the Wisp, he takes them over hedges and ditches, and sometimes round and round the same field, from which they in vain try to find their way back home (although they can always see the path close at hand)…"

It must be said that this parallels the story told to Peter in an almost identical and amazing way; there is the presence of a shape-shifting, magical being, a person whose ability to negotiate familiar pathways is curiously and severely affected, and a clear view of their destination, despite being completely unable to reach it.

Similarly, W.Y. Evans-Wentz, in his definitive study of fairy-lore, *The Fairy Faith in Celtic Countries*, published in 1911, quoted the words of one William Rowe, at the time eighty-two years old, who told the author, "People would go out at night and lose their way and then declare that they had been pisky-led. I think they meant by this that they fell under some spiritual influence—that some spirit led them astray."

Upon hearing of Gabriela's story, and already keenly aware of the legends of people becoming pisky-led in old England, my suspicions that the Puerto Rican chupacabra was, and still is, a beast of definitively paranormal origins, regardless of how we define that emotive word, "paranormal," increased significantly. It was a satisfyingly weird finale to a near nonstop two days of flights, interviews, and treks through El Yunque. I thanked Peter for his time, exited the St. Germain Bistro and Café, took a taxi to Luis Munoz Marin International Airport, and finally, a flight back to Dallas.

Chapter 28

A PHOTOGRAPH FALLS
FLAT ON ITS FACE

My August 2013 trek around Puerto Rico with Galafilm Productions turned out not to be my only exposure to the chupacabra phenomenon that month. Not long after I got back from
the island, the bloodsucker and I crossed paths yet again, in a
most odd way. And, also again, it was all thanks to the world of
television. The researcher who called me said they were planning to make a series, for one of the "big channels" is how it
was described to me, that would focus on a search for ancient
treasures, hidden cities, lost lands, and priceless missing arti-
facts. It was, then, to be a kind of real-life Indiana Jones–type
series. So, what did that have to do with my work in the field of
the chupacabra? Well, it went like this…

The company had somehow got its hands on a photograph
of what appeared to be a crashed old aircraft in the wilds of
Puerto Rico. The excited researcher said the photograph was accompanied by a story. And what a story it was. No one, apparently, knew precisely where the shell of the aircraft was located in

Puerto Rico, only that it was somewhere deep within El Yunque. And, if the lost plane could be found, it would blow the whole chupacabra mystery wide open. I asked: how, exactly, might it do that?

The woman at the other end of the line said they had a story, from a respected and trustworthy source in Puerto Rico, to the effect that at the time of the alleged crash, the crew of the aircraft was in the process of secretly transporting no less than five living and extremely dangerous chupacabras to a military base in the United States. Something, however, went wrong—terribly wrong.

Not long after taking to the late night skies from the old Roosevelt Roads base, ground personnel received frantic communications from the crew to the effect that one of the creatures had broken out of its cage and was rampaging wildly in the body of the plane, which had been specially converted to allow for the cages to be placed on-board. The next thing that was heard was terrible screaming in the cockpit, then nothing but silence and the sudden vanishing of the aircraft from the military's radar screens. Despite an intense search, the aircraft was never found, which I found to be rather baffling. On an island the size of Puerto Rico, a fairly large aircraft crashes and the finest technology of Uncle Sam can't find it?

Then the researcher got to the point. Their contact had told them that as strong and as ruthless as chupacabras are said to be, it was unlikely that even they could have survived a tumultuous aircraft crash in the wilds of Puerto Rico. If the priceless treasure, the skeletal remains of the monsters that just might still be strewn around the rusted body of the aircraft, could be found, the mystery of the chupacabra would be revealed and the existence of the creature would be proved. Yes, the stakes really were that high. I was then asked whether I'd be interested in trekking through El Yunque to try and find the plane. Well, sure I would. It was then, however, that things began to unravel.

I Break the Bad News

I asked if I could see the photograph of the plane. That was not a problem. Within seconds I was looking, on my laptop, at a high-resolution JPEG of what looked like the sort of aircraft that CIA agents would have used to secretly fly nighttime missions in and out of Laos at the height of the Vietnam War. As the photo showed, the plane was in a severely bad state: the wings were gone, what was left was covered in grime, and the dense, surrounding, green vegetation threatened to overwhelm the old fuselage. That was great, right? Nope. It was time for me to share some bad news—some very bad news, actually.

I told the researcher that the story she and her company had been given was pure and unadulterated bullshit. It turns out that, in decidedly synchronistic and fortuitous fashion, I had actually seen the aircraft myself, up close and personal, no less, years before. It was when I traveled to Puerto Rico in September 2005 with Paul Kimball's Red Star Films company to make the *Fields of Fear* documentary for Canada's Space Channel. And the aircraft had not crashed or even crash-landed. It had been owned by a company that years earlier shuttled vacationers back and forth between San Juan and Miami, Florida. At some point, the company went broke and the aircraft was sold off to someone else. Then, eventually, when it became too costly to keep its aging form running, it was left to rot where it stood, which was not in the wilds of El Yunque but actually quite close to a pleasant little town.

As evidence of this, within an hour, I dug out, scanned, and e-mailed my very own photo of the plane taken in 2005, which showed a couple of buildings in the background. It was clear that whoever took the picture which had now got the production company frothing at the mouth had done so very skillfully, and in a way that really did make it look like the plane was in the middle of El Yunque.

I commented to the researcher that I hoped her company didn't pay good money for the photo. Her fumbling, stumbling reply strongly suggested to me that yes, the company did pay for it, and I'm guessing the fee was a fairly considerable one. The conversation was terminated quickly. As, I'm assuming, was the plan for the crew to fly to Puerto Rico to check out the plane's remains.

From a crashed plane, to a conspiracy, and, finally, to a hoax!

Part 6

FINAL WORDS AND THEORIES

Chapter 29

A MONSTER, A MOVIE, AND MOSCOW MAYHEM

The chupacabra phenomenon showed no signs of stopping during either 2013 or 2014. As I mentioned earlier, I thought that the 2005 movie *Chupacabra: Dark Seas* was pretty bad. Compared to 2013's *Chupacabra vs. the Alamo*, however, it was an absolute masterpiece of the highest order possible. The latter starred Erik Estrada, who, you may know or remember, made his name in the late-1970s *Starsky and Hutch* rip-off, *CHiPs*.

Estrada's character in the movie, Carlos Seguin, is someone who leads the battle to destroy a pack of vicious chupacabras that have invaded the Texas city of San Antonio, something which leads to a Davy Crockett–style standoff at the Alamo, in which the chaotic canids are wiped out and the Alamo is blown to pieces.

Rarely have I seen worse special effects, rarely have I ever seen such hammy acting, and rarely have I been so pleased and relieved when a movie was finally over. Mercifully, *Chupacabra vs. the Alamo* didn't even run for ninety minutes. After seeing it,

I actually felt sorry for the real chupacabras. Had they known they were being represented by this kind of garbage they would have been pulling their hair out, if they had any hair to pull out. Thankfully, the real-world chupacabras had their revenge when they hit back with a flurry of activity, which provided them with media coverage and sent the movie spiraling into much justified oblivion.

Also in 2013, I appeared on *The Monster Project*, a short-lived series for the Nat Geo WILD channel. I agreed to appear on the show specifically about the subject of my chupacabra investigations, and was soon filmed in woodland on the fringes of San Antonio, Texas. I really shouldn't have agreed, though. The episode ended up being far less about studying the chupacabra phenomenon and far more about poking fun at those who immerse themselves in the subject.

Back in the (Former) USSR

January 2014 saw the action return to Russia. The town of Beloomut, around one hundred and fifty miles southeast of the city of Moscow, had been recently hit hard by a widespread spate of killings of sheep, cattle, and smaller farm animals. As was the case with so many other reports that caught my attention, the Beloomut attacks were dominated by rumors that the killer drained the blood of its victims. Russian authorities soon put a stop to all that talk: "There are no fairytale creatures in the Lukhovitsky district of the Moscow Region," a stern spokesperson for the Agriculture Ministry told the press.

As authoritative as the statement was, it didn't prevent the attacks from continuing, nor did it do much to put to rest the theory that a wild pack of chupacabras was turning Russia into its new hunting grounds.

"It's a Continuing Goat Massacre"

In July 2014, Manila was targeted by something that sounded suspiciously like the chupacabra. In fact, as the media dug into the story, it was discovered that attacks on animals on the island of Concepcion (known to its people as Sibale) had been going on for no less than two years. Although a number of locals expressed their fears that a diabolical werewolf was on the loose, a fear born out of pre-existing beliefs on the island in lycanthropy, combined with the admittedly thought-provoking fact that many of the attacks occurred during a full moon, there were certain things that suggested otherwise. I carefully examined what was known.

The media noted, on July 13 that, "In an attack last Wednesday, nine goats owned by the local village chief, Ulpiano Ebora of San Vicente, were killed. Before this, several of the livestock were killed in the same locale and the adjacent village of Poblacion. In all, twenty-seven animals have been killed over the past few weeks."

"It's a continuing goat massacre happening at the onset of the full moon almost every year since 2012. So far, more than two hundred goats had been massacred by this unknown killer," said Sibale's outraged Mayor Lemuel Cipriano to the press.

I have to say, it was Cipriano's words that caught my eye on this latest development. If a genuine werewolf was the cause, then why was the animal seemingly only focusing on goats? Surely such a savage, violent beast would have had no trouble when it came to tackling something much bigger than the average goat?

There was something else, too. Although the merciless beast tore its prey to pieces, according to the islanders, it also sucked their blood. Within mythology and folklore, it is the vampire and not the werewolf that is a drainer of blood. Yes, indeed, it was looking more and more like my old nemesis had headed to pastures new.

Chapter 30

A BLOODY CONTROVERSY

With the ten years of my investigations into the world of the chupacabra now detailed, it's time to try and figure out what on earth is going on.

One of the most inflammatory claims surrounding the phenomenon of the chupacabra is that the creatures kill their victims by draining them of blood—sometimes, allegedly, all of the blood. Time and again I have heard this assertion, both in Puerto Rico and in Texas. But is it really true? Well, that very much depends on whom you ask. It also depends, to a great extent, on how one interprets the available evidence.

In 2013, Phylis Canion was interviewed by the *Huffington Post*, and commented on this particular issue, in relation to the creature she had stuffed and mounted: "We know the animal that killed the chicken licked the blood. It opens the throat in the jugular. It seems to like the taste of blood, which is interesting because the only animal that is set up to suck blood is the bat."

Well, no, actually, bats are not set up to suck blood. But we'll come back to that particular issue shortly. Meanwhile, let's start with Ken Gerhard. In July 2014, Ken told me that during the course of his many investigations into the Texas chupacabra, time and again he heard stories to the effect that the slain animals were missing blood, from small to fairly large amounts. There was, however, a problem, as Ken noted: "There was a bit of ambiguity about was it the drinking of the blood—lapping it—or the sucking of it. The notion of any animal drinking blood, apart from some gigantic vampire bat, doesn't make a lot of sense, scientifically speaking. So, I was kind of on the fence."

Ambiguity and fence-sitting surround the matter of the blood draining (or blood drinking) elsewhere, too. During the course of my investigations in Puerto Rico, barely a day went by when I didn't hear at least one story of the chupacabra's vampire-like attacks on livestock and other animals. And I can't tell you how many times the words "blood" and "draining" (or "sucking") were used in the very same sentence. Certainly, as I have noted elsewhere in the pages of this book, I uncovered a number of stories from people who claimed their dead animals were subjected to necropsies, and which confirmed that massive blood loss had occurred.

The problem, however, was that I was never able to secure even a single official necropsy report to validate those claims. On the other side of the coin, I have heard more than a few stories suggesting the assumed huge loss of blood was actually due to the blood of the dead animals sinking to the lowest parts of the victims' bodies after death. What appeared to have been evidence of a significant loss of blood may, then, have really been due to nothing more than wild and uninformed misidentification. And on the issue of misinterpretation, it's important to understand the biology and processes involved in those creatures that do dine on blood.

The Closest Things to Count Dracula

When it comes to the matter of animals that ingest and digest blood (a process called hematophagy), you might be surprised just how many there are. The long list includes bedbugs, lampreys, torpedo snails (a type of sea snail), fleas, horseflies, and *Geospiza difficilis septentrionalis*, the "vampire finch" of the Galapagos Islands, which happens to be the only known bird on the planet that supplements its diet with fresh blood. Of course, the most famous of all the blood-drinking animals is the bat. More specifically—the vampire bat. There are no fewer than three kinds of vampire bat: the hairy-legged, the white-winged, and the common vampire bat, all of which have their origins in the New World. Interestingly, and just like the chupacabra, the white-winged vampire has a particular liking of the blood of goats.

Just like its horror-movie counterpart, this particular breed of vampire prefers to spend its time in places dominated by just one thing—darkness. Caverns, tunnels, abandoned buildings, and caves are among the most favorite abodes of the vampire bat. To say that the vampire bat is a unique creature is not an understatement. It uses what are termed thermoreceptors—sensory neurons—to identify those parts of potential prey where the blood is closest to the surface of the skin and easily accessible. In terms of its attacks, and again just like its fictional, horror-movie-based counterparts, the vampire bat very often feeds on creatures that are sleeping, as this makes them far less likely to fight back. The brain of the vampire bat, and primarily the inferior colliculus, which controls how the brain interprets sound, is particularly honed to allow it to detect an animal that is specifically in the sleep state.

Feeding and Fangs

There are other parallels between vampire bats and the likes of the characters in *True Blood* and *The Strain*. To survive, they have to keep drinking blood, endlessly. Studies have shown that vampire bats cannot go for more than approximately forty-eight hours without a significant amount of the red stuff flowing through their systems. Perhaps most fascinating of all is what happens when a vampire bat fails to find fresh blood. It will approach another member of the colony and, in a fashion that is still not fully understood, give a sign that it is in dire need of food. The other bat, in response, will regurgitate tiny amounts of its own recent intake of blood, thus providing its fellow vampire with much-needed nourishment.

Now we come to the most important aspect of the life and feeding activities of the vampire bat. If it shatters some cherished assumptions, that's too damned bad, but contrary to what many people believe, vampire bats do not suck blood. Ever. Instead, when a bat lands on its sleeping prey, it makes a tiny incision with its razor sharp teeth, that provokes the flow of blood, in much the same way that blood flows to the surface of our skin when it's cut. The bat then proceeds to lap the protein-rich blood, rather than suck it.

Rather incredibly, if the skin of the prey is covered in significant amounts of hair, the vampire bat has the ability to use its teeth to "shave" the hair away, thus allowing it to feed easier. Most ingenious of all, Mother Nature has taken steps to ensure the saliva of the vampire bat contains anticoagulants that prevent the blood of its prey from clotting. The blood, as a result, runs and runs—and runs even more.

To demonstrate the sheer speed and ability with which the vampire bat can feed voraciously on its victim, a fully grown specimen can lap around fifty percent of its own body weight in less than half an hour. The vampire bat has a near-unique digestive system that allows its stomach to absorb plasma from the blood. From there, it makes its way to the kidneys and finally to the bladder. It's a very quick process, too. From intake to urination, the passage of time is around one-and-a-half minutes. And, like all of us, when it's done feeding, the vampire bat finds a place to settle down, relax, and let the process of digestion do its thing.

Back to the Chupacabra

So, what kind of a bearing does this have on the chupacabra? Let's start with the Texan version. Major questions still remain unanswered regarding the matters of those huge overbites, odd pouches, and abnormal limb lengths. On the other hand, autopsies of the animals demonstrate not a solitary bit of evidence that their internal organs have mutated to the extent that they have the ability to digest and absorb massive amounts of blood plasma. That's not to say that while in crazed, homicidal states the creatures might not have lapped or drank small amounts of the blood of their victims; they may well have. But to classify them as animals that can drain, suck, or specifically live on, blood would be very wrong.

As for the Puerto Rican original, unlike its Lone Star State equivalent, we lack a corpse, even a single, solitary one, to examine. Until the day comes or, even, if it comes, when we finally do have a specimen that can be studied carefully, we cannot say for sure what the creature may be capable of. Perhaps, not unlike a vampire bat, it laps up the blood of its victims. And maybe it does so in such a fast, voracious process that enormous quantities of blood are extracted and digested. Perhaps this is what has led to the theory that the Puerto Rican chupacabra sucks the blood of those it kills. Right now, all we can say for sure is that there appears to be a blood-based component to the killings. But the extent to which in Puerto Rico that component mirrors the world of what most people consider to be classic vampirism is something likely to remain a matter of deep debate.

A Monstrous Mutant

One of the most fascinating theories for what the Texas chupacabras might really be comes from Ken Gerhard. While there is no doubt whatsoever in Ken's mind that the creatures are canids, he isn't convinced by the theory that they're just regular coyotes with a bad case of mange and nothing else. It's here that we have to turn our attentions to two specific and controversial issues: industrial pollution and subsequent, bizarre mutation. That there's a distinct possibility the beast of Texas is one born out of man's reckless behavior is ironic. Why so? Let's see.

A favorite movie of both Ken and I is *Prophecy*, a 1979 horror flick that deals with these very issues. Starring Robert Foxworth, *Prophecy* focuses on the rise of monstrous, murderous creatures in the forests that surround the Androscoggin River in Maine. They are regular animals mutated into hideous beasts by exposure to mercury. While the movie certainly takes more than a few liberties when it comes to the science behind genetic mutation, it is a fact that mercury is what is termed a mutagen. That's to say, exposure to mercury can provoke genetic changes at a DNA level, sometimes severe changes. While Ken is not of the opinion that mercury has given rise to the Texas chupacabra, he doesn't rule out the possibility that something similar to the scenario portrayed in *Prophecy* just might have occurred, as incredible as it may sound.

In July 2014, I interviewed Ken on this very issue. What he had to say is as disturbing as it is thought provoking.

The Rise of the Mutants

"Going back to 2004," Ken began, "and right after the reports of the Elmendorf Beast came out, state biologists came out with this sarcoptic mange theory, that these animals, like the Elmendorf Beast and the Pollok animal, were just mangy coyotes. The way that it was explained, it made a lot of sense, initially, because they explained how the bodies of these mangy animals will go through all kinds of extreme changes. Without the hair, they appear to shrink, somewhat. They're very emaciated, so their teeth look larger, their claws look much larger, and so forth."

It's important to note that, in our interview, Ken stressed the word "initially." Certainly, as both time and his investigations progressed, he came around to the idea that while mange certainly seems to play a role in the matter, it's not so cut and dried as the biologists and zoologists would have us believe. Ken told me where his mind is at today on this particular issue:

To my eyes, they didn't look mangy because, typically, with mange you have an animal that has patches of hair, and not something that's completely hairless. Yes, the Elmendorf Beast does have a very slight Mohawk or fringe, which seems to be going down the back parts of their bodies. But, in 2008, I had the opportunity to examine the remains of about a half dozen animals. To my eye, it didn't really seem like mange, because they weren't covered in scars. They weren't bloody. The skin seemed uniformly rough and leathery, but I didn't see any evidence of the scratching and irritation.

Ken continued:

There are, as you know, a handful of other physical abnormalities that have been related to these Texas chupacabras that don't necessarily tie in with the mange theory. Some of them seem to have deformed overbites on their mandibles. There are claims of them having disproportionate limbs. I have photographs where it looks like the hind limbs might be slightly longer than their forelimbs. [They have] marsupial-like sacks on their hind quarters, on their haunches, abnormal numbers of nipples, and very strange, steely blue eyes, almost as if they had cataracts. These abnormalities pop up occasionally, but not consistently.

Ken then got to the crux of his theory:

Now, talking about the pollution aspect, the thing that has always amazed me about these so-called Texas chupacabras is why had we never heard of them before 2004? And why are there so many of them popping up, in the past decade, all over the place, with increasing regularity? That's why I began to wonder if there could be some kind of ecological component, pollution or something else that's causing these animals to appear this way.

If you remember, back in 1995, there were an incredibly large number of deformed frogs found in a pond in southwest Minnesota. It made big national news. It was kind of looked at as a sign of the times: there was so much pollution that man's impact on the environment was causing these really bizarre frog mutations, where they would have extra limbs, missing limbs, weird eyes, and things like that. So, it has occurred to me over the past couple of years that perhaps we're looking at something very similar here in Texas.

Ken Gerhard: pollution and mutagens.

I most certainly did remember the Minnesota mutations. Such was the concern surrounding this series of bizarre, genetic and physical changes in the frog population, none other than the U.S. government's Department of the Interior U.S. Geological Survey undertook careful and concerned studies. Its staff noted on its website:

> Malformed frogs first became the topic of national news in August 1995 when students at a middle school in southern Minnesota discovered one-half of all the frogs they caught in a nearby pond were malformed. Since then, malformed frogs have been reported throughout Minnesota and elsewhere in the United States and Canada.

As the USGS said, the mutations were downright weird: "Malformations included missing limbs, missing digits, extra limbs, partial limbs, skin webbing, malformed jaws, and missing or extra eyes."

On the matter of how exactly the mutations might have occurred, the USGS had a few ideas. All of them were controversial and disturbing:

> Pesticides are known to cause malformation or death of frogs when present in sufficient concentrations. Studies in Canada show a relation between the percentage of malformed frogs and pesticide use. Methoprene, an insecticide widely used to control mosquitoes, also has been suspected as having caused malformations. Endocrine disruptors also are being studied to determine if

they are responsible for some of the frog malformations in Minnesota. Endocrine disruptors are natural and human-made chemicals that interfere with or mimic natural hormones that control development, growth, and behavior of organisms. The number of endocrine disruptors is unknown; only during the last decade has screening of chemicals begun to evaluate endocrine disrupting activity.

The conclusion of the USGS:

> It is likely that one or more combinations of chemical, biological, and physical factors are responsible for causing the malformations in Minnesota frogs. Chemical combinations may be mixtures of natural and human-made organic chemicals, each of which is harmless on its own but toxic when combined. The number of possible combinations of chemicals, biological, and physical factors is enormous, which may explain why finding the causes for frog malformations has been a difficult task.

"This May Be Why They Become Completely Hairless"

Is it feasible that in the same way the frogs of Minnesota were likely mutated via exposure to certain chemicals, such as endocrine disruptors, the Texas chupacabras are coyotes that have been similarly altered, at a physical, genetic level, by exposure to mutagens?

Ken told me in 2014 that this was the direction in which his research and thoughts were now leading him:

Many of these Texas chupacabras have been reported in areas in and around coal-burning power plants. Coal-burning power plants release massive amounts of toxins, including something called sulfur dioxide, which in laboratory tests has been proven to be a mutagen. This is a toxin that can get into an animal's blood makeup and actually cause their cells to mutate. Maybe, as a result of the pollution, the immune systems of these animals have been weakened to the point where, when they do contract the mange mites, their resulting symptoms are much more extreme than anything we've encountered before. This may be why they become completely hairless so fast and why they look so sickly. It might also explain the physical changes, like the forelimb lengths, the overbites, and the pouches.

That the state of Texas is home to around twenty coal-burning plants, alone, is notable. As for sulfur dioxide (also known as SO_2), in 2005 the National Center for Biotechnology Information noted that when, in lab tests, mice were exposed to sulfur dioxide, the outcome was catastrophic: "The results indicate that inhalation exposure to SO_2 damages the DNA of multiple organs in addition to the lung, and suggests that this damage could result in mutation, cancer, and other diseases related to DNA damage."

If pollution and mutation are the answers, should we even be calling the creature a chupacabra? Ken made a few notable comments to me on this particular issue:

I kind of have mixed feelings. I feel that, in some ways, the name "chupacabra" has become so prevalent with regard to these animals that it's almost like a collective name, like they've been anointed as such. And there's no reason, unless we're really sensitive, that we should call them anything else. It's a common name. For example, when I was down in Mexico recently, chasing down Mexican chupacabras and livestock killings down there, the name "chupacabra" came up repeatedly with regard to different types of animals or weird-looking animals that I examined. It struck me that, in Mexico, the name is kind of like a boogeyman—a common name that's associated with any type of mysterious creature or bugaboo. It's a catchall, which, again, goes back to the Texas chupacabra.

But on the other hand, I feel that, as someone who takes a scientific approach, perhaps we're doing it a disservice by promoting that particular myth. And at this point we would be better suited, particularly with regard to cryptozoologists, who catch so much flak anyways, to try and be a bit more technical in our descriptions and refer to them as Texas blue-dogs, the name proposed by the Center for Fortean Zoology.

We are then at least acknowledging that these are canids. They've been DNA-tested and we know definitively that's what they are. But they are physically unusual canids and they deserve their own classification for that reason.

An Unknown Mutation

We're still not finished with mutagens, pollution, and the chupacabra. Jon Downes had something to say on this very matter that was of profound interest to me. It all revolved around a 2009 trip he made to Texas, during which he uncovered something of deep relevance to the theories of Ken Gerhard.

Jon's journey took him to Fayetteville, where he met with a family who for some years had seen strange beasts living in several locations on their ranch. Once they had even found roadkill, which had been sent to a nearby university, but which was unable to identify it. Once again, the description was of blue/grey, hairless, dog-like creatures larger than the largest coyote, with long muzzles and hunched backs.

The family took Jon to a remote part of their ranch where, in the sandy walls of a desolate gulch, there was a series of large holes that led deep into the sandy cliff face. These were, or at least had been, the lair of a family of these creatures, they explained. They had seen them on a number of occasions, including a large specimen that went into a hole and came out again facing the other way, which implied that inside was an area big enough for it to have turned around.

Now we come to the most important part of all. The family, said Jon, had once been the proud owners of a large and fruitful orchard of pecan trees. In recent years, though, they had seen their legacy being slowly but surely destroyed as trees withered and died, and even apparently healthy trees produced few or no nuts. They blamed this upon SO_2 from a local coal-fueled power station. Could it be, they wondered (as did Jon), that these silent but deadly emissions had somehow caused an unknown mutation in one of the canids living in the area and, as a consequence, produced a strain of these strange, bald, blue dogs?

Puerto Rico:
Pollution and Contamination

It's now time to make a very quick trip back to Puerto Rico for the next part of the story of the mutating chupacabra. That Puerto Rico has been the site of numerous, controversial testing of weird concoctions is not in doubt. Herbicide Orange, known far more notoriously as Agent Orange, is a weapon of what is called herbicidal warfare. It was used during the Vietnam War to destroy North Vietnamese crops, as well as to defoliate entire swathes of forest and jungle that the Viet Cong used as cover.

An even more destructive form of Agent Orange, called Super Agent Orange, was secretly tested in Puerto Rico in the 1960s by staff from both the Dugway Proving Ground and Fort Detrick, Maryland (don't forget that whistleblower, Ed, of thylacine infamy, claimed to work at Dugway). It was perfected by Monsanto, a biotech company operating out of St. Louis, Missouri. The *International Journal of Epidemiology* notes: "Parental exposure to Agent Orange appears to be associated with an increased risk of birth defects."

The list of defects is grim: hernias, cleft palates, and mental problems. There's something else too. Remember that story told to Jon Downes and me in 2004, the one that revolved around an entire village of people suffering from something that sounded very much like progeria, but that some of the locals suspected were nothing less than full-blown vampires? You'll recall that some of the people allegedly had extra digits on their hands and feet. Extra fingers and toes in newborns have been reported on numerous occasions in areas hit by Agent Orange, such as North Vietnam and Puerto Rico.

Having reviewed all of the data and chatted with Ken, I found it interesting (and I still do find it interesting) that in both Texas and Puerto Rico, where mutagens and pollution are rife, bizarre-looking, mysterious creatures surfaced, seemingly out of nowhere. That the Puerto Rican chupacabra was widely reported from only 1995 onwards, and that the hairless Texas creatures suddenly started popping up in 2004, led me to think that DNA-scrambling pollutants just might have spawned these mutated things.

Maybe *Prophecy* was not quite the fictional movie that most viewers assumed it to be. It just might have been a perfect example of forecasting the future.

CONCLUSION

My quest to determine the truth of the chupacabra has been an extraordinary and an extraordinarily weird one. Having reviewed all of my old files, notes, interviews, and photos, and having captured all of the relevant data in the pages of this book, it's time for me to try and come to some form of conclusion, a resolution, a closure, if such things are even possible. I'm not altogether sure they are, but I am willing to give it a try.

I guess the first thing I learned, above all else, is that the only way to get the answers is to go looking for them. Yes, the Internet is a great resource tool; it provides a huge amount of data on the chupacabra, whether in the United States, Puerto Rico, or elsewhere. What the Internet does not do and cannot do, however, is to provoke or provide the unique sense of wonder that comes from sitting across from a real living, breathing person who tells you of their face-to-face encounter with something terrifying, deadly, and inhuman.

The Internet is very impersonal, too, in the sense that it has no real ability to encourage people to speak of their encounters. Getting to know the witnesses, gaining their confidence, and demonstrating that your reasons for wanting to discuss and share their experiences are worthwhile and valid ones can really only be achieved in the field, which just happens to be one of my favorite places to hang out.

So what have my ten years of exploration revealed to me? I'd say a hell of a lot. Some of the information that I have uncovered has vindicated my thoughts and theories on the nature of the beasts. Other data has radically altered many of my assumptions and ideas. All of it, however, has allowed me to see that the reality of the situation is far different from that which many have suggested. Has that made the picture any clearer, in regard to what's going on?

The most important thing that my research has demonstrated is that the chupacabra is not definable as one kind of creature or as a single phenomenon. Quite clearly, and despite the widespread assumptions that exist, the Puerto Rican beast is very different from those of Texas, Oklahoma, Mexico, and elsewhere. While both entities have predilections for attacking small animals, the bipedal, spiked, and possibly even winged animal of Puerto Rico is obviously not a hairless, mutated coyote. And vice versa!

So what are we dealing with? In terms of the Texas chupacabra, I truly do believe that Ken Gerhard may well be on the right track with his theories that the Lone Star State's creepy canids could be born out of catastrophic exposure to certain mutagens. We just might be seeing the emergence of a creature that is radically and with phenomenal speed being transformed from its original form into something else.

As far as the Puerto Rican creature is concerned, matters are very different, as I see things anyway.

My extensive time spent on the island has led me to conclude that trying to pinpoint the chupacabra as just one thing is not just impossible, but also disingenuous. That occultists may have exploited the legend of the creature to help mask their secret, sacrificial rites and rituals is something I find to be highly likely. That a number of encounters may have been due to the presence of wild, rogue monkeys, a scenario I came across time and again, is also something I do not dismiss. And that large cats are known to have been on the loose in Puerto Rico suggests to me their predations probably account for at least a few attacks attributed to the chupacabra. The same goes for the huge presence of wild dogs on the island. But there's clearly far more afoot, too.

Despite what the naysayers might spout, I absolutely believe that a core body of reports does demonstrate the presence of a genuinely unknown creature in Puerto Rico. A number of accounts still stand out for me, years after I was first exposed to them. It's difficult to suggest any kind of conventional explanation for the creatures that the witnesses encountered and were confronted by at such close quarters, giving them the ability to see the beasts right before their very eyes.

Then there are those conspiratorial stories that so often came my way, those of a connection between the chupacabra and Roosevelt Roads, the crashed UFO associations, that extremely bizarre story of genetically mutated thylacines, and that mysterious village overwhelmed by progeria. Are they simply modern-day myths, friend-of-a-friend tales, and the kinds of stories that surface and flourish just about everywhere in the face of deep mystery, fear, paranoia, and hysteria? They might well be. On the other hand, perhaps somewhere deep inside these twisting, tumultuous tales, there is a truth—perhaps several, maybe even many, truths.

To a great extent, the chupacabra mystery remains shrouded in mystery, intrigue, secrecy, and legend. There is one thing, however, that I do know for sure: it won't be long before I'm back on the trail of that marauding and deadly beast, seeking it out, unraveling the questions of what it is (or what they really are), and trying my damndest to put the mystery to rest.

Whether doing so will require the use of science and technology or a wooden stake through the heart, a more-than-liberal sprinkling of garlic, and the brandishing of a silver cross still remains to be seen.

BIBLIOGRAPHY

Author's Note: All web addresses were checked for accuracy in May 2015.

"Alien Big Cats." http://www.unexplained-mysteries.com/viewarticle.php?id=2. 2014.

"Animal Symbolism: Meaning of Coyote." http://www.whats-your-sign.com/animal-symbolism-coyote.html. 2014.

Ardizzoni, Susan. "Texas State University Researcher Helps Unravel Mystery of Texas 'Blue Dog' Claimed to be Chupacabra." http://bionews-tx.com/news/2013/09/01/texas-state-university-researcher-helps-unravel-mystery-of-texas-blue-dog-claimed-to-be-chupacabra/. September 1, 2013.

"At Wind Chimes Inn." http://www.atwindchimesinn.com/. 2014.

Carey, Thomas J., and Donald R. Schmitt. *Inside the Real Area 51: The Secret History of Wright-Patterson*. Pompton Plains, N.J.: New Page Books, 2013.

"Caribbean Primate Research Center." http://cprc.rcm.upr.edu/. 2014.

Cawthon Lang, Kristina. "Rhesus macaque." http://pin.primate.wisc.edu/factsheets/entry/rhesus_macaque. July 20, 2005.

"Ceiba, Puerto Rico." http://www.icoquito.com/puerto-rico-articles/ceiba-puerto-rico/. 2014.

Childress, David Hatcher. "Living Pterodactyls Haunt Our Skies." http://educate-yourself.org/cn/PterodactylsHauntSkies30mar05.shtml. March 30, 2005.

"Chupacabra Headquarters: About the Chupacabra." http://www.cuerochupacabra.com/id1.html. 2014.

"Chupacabra vs. The Alamo." http://www.syfy.com/movies/chupacabra_vs_the_alamo. 2014.

Colangelo, Lisa L., and Melissa Grace. "Staten Island pa turns in son after sicko attack on peacock." http://www.nydailynews.com/news/crime/staten-island-pa-turns-son-sicko-attack-peacock-article-1.265918. July 2, 2007.

"Common Vampire Bat." http://animals.nationalgeographic.com/animals/mammals/common-vampire-bat/. 2014.

Corrales, Scott. *Chupacabras and Other Mysteries*. Murfreesboro, TN: Greenleaf Publications, 1997.

Corrales, Scott. "Nemesis: The Chupacabras at Large." http://www.scribd.com/doc/139738026/NEMESIS-The-Chupacabras-at-Large-Reissue-2013. 2013.

Corrales, Scott. "The Moca Vampire." http://www.meta- religion.com/Paranormale/Cryptozoology/Other/ moca_vampire.htm#.U_dQUGOEeSo. January 19, 2007.

Courtney, Margaret Ann. *Cornish Feasts and Folklore*. London, U.K.: Beare & Son, 1890.

Currey, Cecil B. *Edward Lansdale: The Unquiet American*. Boston, MA: Houghton Mifflin, 1989.

"Dark Side of Santeria, The: Palo Mayombe." http://www.palomayombe.net/About_Us.html. 2014.

Deane, Zain. "San Juan Neighborhoods. Guide to Rio Piedras." http://gopuertorico.about.com/od/sanjuan/p/RioPiedras.htm. 2014.

Diaz, Lily. "A Structuralist Analysis of Puerto Rican Santeria." http://www.t0.or.at/0ntext/ldsanter.htm. 1996.

"Diseases and Conditions: Progeria." http://www.mayoclinic.org/diseases-conditions/progeria/basics/definition/con-20029424. 2014.

"Do the Grays Have Progeria?" http://x-gumis.klub.chip.pl/Reszta/ufo_eng/progeria.htm. 2014.

Downes, Jonathan. *Only Fools and Goat Suckers*. Woolsery, U.K.: CFZ Press, 2001.

———. "Texas Blue Dogs." *Fortean Times*, February 2012.

———. *The Island of Paradise: Chupacabra, UFO Crash Retrievals, and Accelerated Evolution on the Island of Puerto Rico*. Woolsery, U.K.: CFZ Press, 2008.

Dr. Chills. "Mimic (1997) Review." http://www.best-horror-movies.com/review?name=mimic-1997-review. July 7, 2012.

Drake, Frank, and Dava Sobel. *Is Anyone Out There?* New York: Delacorte Press, 1992.

Eddleman, Jo Ann. "Coleman Municipal Airport." http://www.colemantexas.org/airport.html. 2014.

"El Yunque National Forest, 2002 Wildlife Facts: Bats." http://www.fs.usda.gov/detail/elyunque/learning/nature-science/?cid=fsbdev3_043047. 2002.

Ellsworth, Ken. "Coleman residents question shooting of fabled monkey." *Ellsworth County Independent Reporter*, December 1, 2000.

"Elmendorf Beast." http://www.redorbit.com/education/reference_library/general-2/cryptozoology/1112911319/elmendorf-beast/. 2014.

Evans-Wentz, W.Y. *The Fairy Faith in Celtic Countries*. Pompton Plains, NJ: New Page Books, 2004.

Evora, Robert A. "Werewolves kill herds of animals in Sibale island." http://manilastandardtoday.com/2014/07/11/werewolves-kill-herds-of-animals-in-sibale-island/. July 11, 2014.

Gannon, Michael R. (editor). *Bats of Puerto Rico: An Island Focus and a Caribbean Perspective*. Lubbock, TX: Texas Tech University Press, 2005.

Gerhard. Ken. "Beware the Elmendorf Beast!" http://blogs.sacur-rent.com/streetview/beware-the-elmendorf-beast/. April 8, 2011.

Gerhard, Ken, and Nick Redfern. *Monsters of Texas*. Woolsery, U.K: CFZ Press, 2010.

Gonzalez-Wippler, Migene. *Santeria: the Religion*. Woodbury, MN: Llewellyn Publications, 2002.

Goolsby, Dana. "Blood Sucking Chupacabras, Mutants, and Mangy Coyotes—Oh My!" http://myetx.com/blood-sucking-chupaca-bras-mutants-and-mangy-coyotes-oh-my/. September 21, 2011.

Greene, Graham. *Our Man in Havana*. London, U.K.: Penguin Classics, 2007.

Gwenn. "Not So Usual Sights in Old San Juan." http://www.puer-toricodaytrips.com/unusual-osj-sights/. July 15, 2012.

Harpur, Merrily. *Mystery Big Cats*. Loughborough, U.K.: Heart of Albion Press, 2006.

Inexplicita. "Puerto Rico: The Gargoyle vs. The Chupacabras." http://inexplicata.blogspot.com/2010/08/puerto-rico-gargoyle-vs-chupacabras.html. August 30, 2010.

"Investigation leads to more Chupacabras." http://www.lostworld-museum.com/2006/11/34-investigation-leads-to-more-chupaca-bras/. November 15, 2006.

"Jonathan Downes Hunts Chupacabra, Part 1." https://www.you-tube.com/watch?v=mf3LzXdwvb4. April 11, 2011.

"Jonathan Downes Hunts Chupacabra, Part 2." https://www.you-tube.com/watch?v=WMdWbvzRrbE. April 11, 2011.

Keeson, Arvid. "Dugway Mysteries Revealed—The New Area 51." http://www.utahstories.com/2012/10/dugway-myteries-re-vealed-the-new-area-51/. October 12, 2012.

Kunzelman, Michael. "Court hears Texas case over Santeria animal sacrifices." http://usatoday30.usatoday.com/news/religion/2009-04-01-santeria-sacrifices_N.htm. April 1, 2009.

Lansdale, Edward G. *In the Midst of Wars: An American's Mission to Southeast Asia*. Bronx, New York: Fordham University Press, 1991.

"Legendary Native American Figures: Coyote the Trickster (Southwest)." http://www.native-languages.org/southwest-coyote.htm. 2014.

Lennox, Sean. "Texas Chupacabra: Living Chupacabra May Have Been Caught." http://www.ecanadanow.com/curiosity/2014/04/04/texas-chupacabra-living-chupacabra-may-have-been-caught/. April 4, 2014.

"Live Pterosaur. Category: Mexico Sightings." http://www.livepterosaur.com/LP_Blog/archives/category/mexico-sightings. 2014.

"Macaque shot in Coleman County, Texas." https://groups.yahoo.com/neo/groups/APES/conversations/topics/6765. December 4, 2000.

"Malformed Frogs in Minnesota: An Update." http://pubs.usgs.gov/fs/fs-043-01/. February 18, 2014.

Malten, Willem. "The Case Against Agent Orange And All Mutagenic Weapons." http://truth-out.org/archive/component/k2/item/71210:the-case-against-agent-orange-and-all-mutagenic-weapons. June 14, 2007.

Miller, Michael E. "Puerto Rico's Wave of Drugs and Brazen Murders Reverberates to Miami." http://www.miaminewtimes.com/2013-03-21/news/puerto-rico-drugs-murders-miami/full/. March 21, 2013.

"Monster Project, The. Episode: Chupacabra." http://channel.nationalgeographic.com/wild/the-monster-project/episodes/chupacabra/. 2014.

Moscow Regional Officials Formally Deny Existence of Chupacabra." http://en.ria.ru/russia/20140125/186890180/Moscow-Region-Officials-Formally-Deny-Existence-of-Chupacabra.html. January 25, 2014.

Moye, David. "Phylis Canion Captures Texas Blue Dog, Possible Chupacabra On 'The Unexplained Files.'" http://www.huffingtonpost.com/2013/08/27/phylis-canion_n_3805887.html. August 27, 2013.

Muir, John Kenneth. "Cult Movie Review: Prophecy (1979)." http://
reflectionsonfilmandtelevision.blogspot.com/2013/01/cult-mov-
ie-review-prophecy-1979.html. January 4, 2013.

"Mutagen." https://www.princeton.edu/~achaney/tmve/wiki100k/
docs/Mutagen.html. 2014.

Nashel, Jonathan. *Edward Lansdale's Cold War*. Amherst, MA: University of Massachusetts Press, 2005.

"National Park Mysteries Trailer." https://www.youtube.com/
watch?v=uEBa5P9VDns. May 10, 2013.

Nino, Mark. "Okie Chupacabras." http://www.kveo.com/national/
okie-chupacabras. July 23, 2010.

"Panther or Puerto Rican Chupacabras?" http://www.cryptozoon-
ews.com/panther-pr-chup/. 2014.

"Peacock Symbolism and Meaning." http://www.whats-your-sign.
com/peacock-symbolism.html. 2014.

Platt, James. "Blood-sucking chupacabra goes on rampage in Russian villages." http://english.pravda.ru/science/mysteries/27-
04-2006/79616-chupacabra-0/. April 27, 2006.

"Ponce." http://welcome.topuertorico.org/city/ponce.shtml. 2014.

"Proof Positive: Evidence of the Paranormal." http://www.imdb.
com/title/tt0423716/. 2014.

"Pteronotus quadridens." http://prgap.org/species/pteronotus-
quadridens/. 2014.

"Puerto Rico Killing Troublesome Monkeys." http://www.nbcnews.
com/id/28317943/ns/world_news-world_environment/t/
puerto-rico-killing-troublesome-monkeys/#.U_oIHmOEeSo.
December 19, 2008.

"Puerto Rican Officials Hunt Black Panther Prowling Suburbs."
http://www.foxnews.com/story/2008/12/14/puerto-rican-offi-
cials-hunt-black-panther-prowling-suburbs/. December 14, 2008.

"Puerto Rico: A Timeline." http://www.pbs.org/wgbh/master-
piece/americancollection/woman/timeline.html. 2014.

"Puerto Rico Mystery—11 Goats Slain in Petting Zoo." http://www.
rense.com/general60/goats.htm. December 3, 2004.

Radford, Ben. *Tracking the Chupacabra: The Vampire Beast in Fact, Fiction, and Folklore*. Albuquerque, NM: University of New Mexico Press, 2011.

"Real-Life Blood Suckers." http://blog.3bscientific.com/science_education_insight/2013/10/real-life-blood-suckers.html. October 18, 2013.

Redfern, Nick. "Creature of the Month: The Werecat of Britain." http://newpagebooks.blogspot.com/2014/04/creature-of-month-werecat-of-britain-by.html. April 24, 2014.

Redfern, Nick. Interview with Ken Gerhard, July 14, 2014.

Redfern, Nick. Interview with Paul Kimball, August 20, 2014.

Redfern, Nick. "Lair of the Beasts: The Bodalog Monster." http://www.mania.com/lair-beasts-bodalog-monster_article_122821.html. May 29, 2010.

Redfern, Nick. "Peacock High-Strangeness." http://nickredfern-fortean.blogspot.com/2012/09/peacock-high-strangeness.html. September 6, 2012.

"Riot Police Evict 300 Squatters In Puerto Rico." *Palm Beach Post*, May 19, 1982.

"Roosevelt Roads History And Facts." http://www.rrhsalumni.com/rooseyhistoryfacts.htm. 2014.

"Roosevelt Roads Naval Station." http://www.globalsecurity.org/military/facility/roosevelt-roads.htm. 2014.

Sinpetru, Laura. "Chupie, the Texas Chupacabra, Has Been Put to Sleep." http://news.softpedia.com/news/Chupie-the-Texas-Chupacabra-Has-Been-Put-to-Sleep-436035.shtml. April 5, 2014.

Soniak, Matt. "11 Bloody Facts About Vampire Bats." http://mentalfloss.com/article/53128/11-bloody-facts-about-vampire-bats. October 11, 2013.

"Stewart, Will. "Fabled 'Chupacabra' or mutant fox poisoned by radiation?" http://www.dailymail.co.uk/news/article-2192561/Fabled-Chupacabra-mutant-fox-poisoned-radiation-Russian-hunters-baffled-dog-like-animal.html. August 23, 2012.

"Supreme Court on Santeria." http://userwww.sfsu.edu/biella/santeria/dec1.html. 2014.

Switek, Brian. "You Say 'Velociraptor,' I say 'Deinonychus.'" http://
www.smithsonianmag.com/science-nature/you-say-velociraptor-
i-say-deinonychus-33789870/?no-ist. November 7, 2008.

"Tasmania Tiger, The." http://australia.gov.au/about-australia/
australian-story/tasmanian-tiger. July 12, 2007.

"Texas 2010." http://texasbluedogs.blogspot.com/. 2010.

"Texas Chupacabra." http://roswellbooks.com/museum/?page_
id=497. 2014.

"Thylacine, or Tasmanian Tiger, *Thylacinus cynocephalus*." http://
www.parks.tas.gov.au/indeX.aspX?base=4765. June 18, 2010.

Torres, Luis. "Puerto Rico: U.S. Lab." http://vigilantcitizen.com/vc-
community/puerto-rico-us-lab/. March 18, 2014.

"Treaty on Principles Governing the Activities of States in the Exploration and Use of Outer Space, Including the Moon and Other
Celestial Bodies." http://www.state.gov/t/isn/5181.htm. 2014.

Tresca, Michael. "Chupacabra: Dark Seas." http://www.examiner.
com/article/chupacabra-dark-seas. August 21, 2010.

Turner, Allan. "An often misunderstood faith, Santeria community
thrives here." http://www.houstonchronicle.com/news/houston-
texas/houston/article/An-often-misunderstood-faith-Santeria-
community-5240848.php#/0. February 16, 2014.

"Two chupacabra shot, killed in Dewitt County." http://www.
victoriaadvocate.com/news/2008/aug/30/tb_chupaca-
bra_083108_16565/. August 30, 2008.

"Two Dewitt County sheriff's deputies claiming they tape
a chupacabra on dash cam." http://www.liveleak.com/
view?i=a13_1218564871. 2014.

"Velociraptor Mongoliensis." http://animals.nationalgeographic.
com/animals/prehistoric/velociraptor-mongoliensis/. 2014.

"Visit an Island run by Monkeys." *http://www.puertoricodaytrips.com/
monkey-island/*. December 16, 2008.

"Walter H. Andrus, Jr." http://www.paradigmresearchgroup.org/
Hall%20of%20Fame/Andrus_Walter.htm. 2005.

Washington, Tom. "'Vampire' stalks Siberian livestock." http://
themoscownews.com/russia/20110726/188875163.html. July 26,
2011.

Weaver, Gordon. *Conan Doyle and the Parson's Son: The George Edalji Case.* Cambridge, U.K.: Vanguard Press, 2006.

Winthrop, Lynn. "'Zombie Dog' Puzzles Experts." http://www.fvza.
org/prchupacabra.html. October 12, 2004.

"Yenaldlooshi." http://www.demonicpedia.com/demons/american-
demons/yenaldlooshi/. January 26, 2014.

Acknowledgments

I would like to offer my very sincere thanks to all of the following:

Ken Gerhard, for generously sharing with me his thoughts and theories on the chupacabra—of both Texas and Puerto Rico; Jonathan Downes, with whom it was a privilege and a joy to spend a week in Puerto Rico in search of vampires; Paul Kimball, for inviting me along on his expedition to find out the truth of the chupacabra; my tireless literary agent, Lisa Hagan, without whom you would not be reading this book; everyone at Llewellyn Publications, but particularly Amy Glaser, Kathy Schneider, Kat Sanborn, and Jennifer Ackman; Shane Van Boxtel, for the photograph of me that accompanies my biography; and, finally, all of those people who generously shared with me their stories, accounts, and ideas on—and encounters with—the chupacabra.

To Write the Author

If you wish to contact the author or would like more information about this book, please write to the author in care of Llewellyn Worldwide, and we will forward your request. Both the author and publisher appreciate hearing from you and learning of your enjoyment of this book and how it has helped you. Llewellyn Worldwide cannot guarantee that every letter written to the author can be answered, but all will be forwarded. Please write to:

Nick Redfern
℅ Llewellyn Worldwide
2143 Wooddale Drive
Woodbury, MN 55125-2989

Please enclose a self-addressed stamped envelope for reply,
or $1.00 to cover costs. If outside the U.S.A., enclose
an international postal reply coupon.